ULTIMATE MEAL PREP

COOKBOOK

Be One Step Ahead of Your Daily Meals With 77 Easy and Delicious Recipes to Maintain a Healthy Lifestyle and Lose Weight.

MEAL PREP COOKBOOK HEALTHY

MEAL PREP COOKBOOK LOW CARB

MEAL PREP COOKBOOK

HEALTHY

Table of Contents

INTRODUCTION

A healthy diet is fundamental for acceptable wellbeing and nourishment. It secures you against numerous constant no communicable illnesses, like coronary illness, diabetes and disease. Eating an assortment of food varieties and devouring less salt, sugars and immersed and mechanically delivered trans-fats, are fundamental for healthy diet.

What we eat can influence every one of the cycles in the body, including cell recovery, irritation, assimilation and rest. So it's nothing unexpected that after even just 28 days of eating great you can hope to look better, yet feel a ton better, as well. Healthy meals highlights organic products, vegetables, entire grains, and sans fat or low-fat milk and milk items incorporates an assortment of protein food sources like fish, lean meats and poultry, eggs, vegetables (beans and peas), soy items, nuts, and seeds is low in soaked fats, Trans fats, cholesterol, salt (sodium), and added sugars.

This book contains such recipes which have part of medical advantages. Inside seven days of eating better, you'll notice that your energy level has gone up. You'll be improving rest and dealing with every one of the exercises of the day like a professional. Odds are, you will not feel very bloated.

1. Roasted Chicken and Vegetables

Total Time: 1 hr. | Prep: 15 min. | Bake: 45 min. |
Makes 6 servings

INGREDIENTS

- 2 pounds red potatoes (around 6 medium), cut into 3/4-inch pieces
- 1 enormous onion, coarsely chopped
- 2 tablespoons olive oil
- 3 garlic cloves, minced
- 1-1/4 teaspoons salt, separated
- 1 teaspoon dried rosemary, squashed, isolated
- 3/4 teaspoon pepper, separated
- 1/2 teaspoon paprika
- 6 bone-in chicken thighs (around 2-1/4 pounds), skin eliminated
- 6 cups new child spinach (around 6 ounces)

DIRECTIONS

1. Preheat oven to 425°. In a huge bowl, consolidate potatoes, onion, oil, garlic, 3/4 teaspoon salt, 1/2 teaspoon rosemary and 1/2 teaspoon pepper; throw to cover. Move to a 15x10x1-in. preparing pan covered with cooking shower.

2. In a small bowl, blend paprika and the leftover salt, rosemary and pepper. Sprinkle chicken with paprika combination; organize over vegetables. Cook until a thermometer embedded in chicken peruses 170°-175° and vegetables are simply delicate, 35-40 minutes.

3. Eliminate chicken to a serving platter; keep warm. Top vegetables with spinach. Broil until vegetables are delicate and spinach is shriveled, 8-10 minutes longer. Mix vegetables to join; present with chicken.

4. Set up your sheet-pan supper the prior night and simply pop it into the preheated oven to prepare. This serves to profoundly enhance the chicken, a shared benefit!

5. In the event that you need a more extravagant dish, use skin-on chicken, and on the off chance that you need a lighter dish, utilize

bone-in chicken breasts. Make certain to cook bone-in breasts just to 165-170 degrees, since more slender meat can get dry at higher temperatures.

2. Ham Steaks with Gruyere, Bacon & Mushrooms

Total Time Prep/Total Time: 25 min. Makes 4 servings

INGREDIENTS

- 2 tablespoons spread
- 1/2 pound cut new mushrooms
- 1 shallot, finely chopped
- 2 garlic cloves, minced
- 1/8 teaspoon coarsely ground pepper
- 1 completely cooked boneless ham steak (around 1 pound), cut into 4 pieces
- 1 cup shredded Gruyere cheddar
- 4 bacon strips, cooked and disintegrated
- 1 tablespoon minced new parsley, optional

DIRECTIONS

1. In an enormous nonstick skillet, heat spread over medium-high heat. Add mushrooms and shallot; cook and mix 4-6 minutes or until delicate. Add garlic and pepper; cook brief longer. Eliminate from pan; keep warm. Wipe skillet clean.

2. In same skillet, cook ham over medium heat 3 minutes. Turn; sprinkle with cheddar and bacon. Cook, covered, 2-4 minutes longer or until cheddar is softened and ham is heated through. Present with mushroom blend. Whenever wanted, sprinkle with parsley.

3. Lemony Parsley Baked Cod

Total Time Prep/Total Time: 25 min. Makes 4 servings

INGREDIENTS

- 3 tablespoons minced fresh parsley
- 2 tablespoons lemon juice
- 1 tablespoon grated lemon zest
- 1 tablespoon olive oil
- 2 garlic cloves, minced
- 1/4 teaspoon salt
- 1/8 teaspoon pepper
- 4 cod fillets (6 ounces each)
- 2 green onions, chopped

DIRECTIONS

1. Preheat oven to 400°. In a small bowl, mix the first seven INGREDIENTS. Place cod in an ungreased 11x7-in. baking dish; top with parsley mixture. Drizzle with green onions. Bake, covered, 10-15 minutes or until fish flakes easily with a fork.

4. Easy Firehouse Chili

Total Time Prep: 20 min. Cook: 1-1/2 hours Makes 16 servings (4 quarts)

INGREDIENTS

- 2 tablespoons canola oil
- 4 pounds lean ground hamburger (90% lean)
- 2 medium onions, chopped
- 1 medium green pepper, chopped
- 4 jars (16 ounces every) kidney beans, washed and depleted
- 3 jars (28 ounces each) stewed tomatoes, cut up
- 1 can (14-1/2 ounces) hamburger stock
- 3 tablespoons bean stew powder
- 2 tablespoons ground coriander
- 2 tablespoons ground cumin

- 4 garlic cloves, minced
- 1 teaspoon dried oregano

DIRECTIONS

1. In a Dutch oven, heat canola oil over medium heat. Brown hamburger in clumps, disintegrating meat, until not, at this point pink; channel and put in a safe spot. Add onions and green pepper; cook until delicate. Return meat to Dutch oven. Mix in excess INGREDIENTS. Heat to the point of boiling. Diminish heat; stew, covered, until flavors are mixed, around 1-1/2 hours.

2. Canola oil is high in monounsaturated fat, a sort that assists with diminishing blood cholesterol levels, and low in immersed fat, which can build blood cholesterol. Olive oil would likewise taste extraordinary in this formula and has similar solid fat properties.

3. Lean ground turkey (93% lean) contains 53% less fat and 38% less soaked fat than ordinary ground turkey (85% lean). It works extraordinary in goulashes, tacos and different dishes that utilization disintegrated meat.

Higher-fat meat turns out better for burgers or meatloaf.

5. Chicken Tequila Fettuccine

INGREDIENTS

- 1-2 pounds dry spinach fettuccine (or 2 pounds fresh)
- 1/2 cup chopped cilantro (2 tablespoons for garnish/finishing)
- 2-tablespoons of chopped fresh garlic
- 2-tablespoons chopped jalapeno pepper (seeds and veins can be removed if a milder flavor is desired)
- 3-tablespoons unsalted butter (reserve tablespoons per container)
- 1/2 cup of chicken stock
- 2-tablespoons of tequila

- 2-tablespoons of freshly squeezed lime juice
- 3-tablespoons of soy sauce
- 1/2 pound chicken breast diced 3/4 inch
- 1/4 cup red onion thinly sliced
- 1 1/2 cup of red bell pepper thinly sliced
- 1/2 cup of yellow bell pepper thinly sliced
- 1/2 cup green pepper thinly sliced
- 1 1/2 cups of cream

DIRECTIONS

1. Quickly prepare to boil salted water for cooking pasta; cook dinner al dente, for dry pasta for 8 to 10 minutes, for bubbly for about three minutes. Pasta can be cooked, rinsed, and oiled slightly ahead of time, after which it is "flashed" in boiling water or cooked to match the sauce/topping.

2. Mix 1/3 cup of cilantro, garlic, and jalapeno over medium heat in 2 tablespoons of oil for four to 5 minutes. Remove lime juice, tequila, and stock. Bring the combination to a boil and cook to a pasty consistency until reduced; put aside.

3. Pour over the diced soy sauce; Set aside for 5 minutes. Meanwhile, prepare evening onions and peppers with the last of butter over medium heat, stirring occasionally. Toss and add the reserved vegetables and cream when the vegetable wilt (go limp), add the chook and soy sauce.

4. Bring the sauce to a boil; cook gently until the chicken has melted and the sauce is thick (about 3 minutes).

6. Salmon-and-Rice Soup

Prep time: 20 min Serving 4

INGREDIENTS

- 3/4 c. long-grain rice
- 1/2 lb. salmon filet
- 2 tbsp. soy sauce
- 1 tbsp. Asian sesame oil
- 10 cilantro stems
- 1/2 tbsp. minced new ginger
- 1 tsp. salt
- 2 c. canned low-sodium chicken stock or natively constructed stock
- 4 c. water
- 3 scallions including green tops

- This fixing shopping module is made and kept up by an outsider, and imported onto this page. You might have the option to discover more data about this and comparative substance on their site.

DIRECTIONS

1. Heat a medium pot of salted water to the point of boiling. Mix in the rice and bubble until practically delicate, around 10 minutes. Channel.
2. Coat the salmon with the soy sauce and sesame oil.
3. In an enormous pot, join the cooked rice, the cilantro stems, the ginger, salt, stock and water. Heat to the point of boiling. Decrease the heat and stew, covered, blending at times, for 15 minutes.
4. Add the salmon to the pot. Stew, covered, until the salmon is simply done, around 5 minutes. Eliminate the cilantro stems. Serve the soup decorated with the cilantro leaves and scallions.

5. Notes: We utilized long-grain rice for our soup. In China and Japan, it would be made with short-grain, which is starchier and disintegrates into the soup all the more promptly. On the off chance that you need to go the short-grain course, Arborio is promptly accessible.

6. Wine Recommendation: Pairing this soup with wine might be somewhat of a stretch. An ale lager is a vastly improved decision. Most awesome aspect all: little jars of warm, tart purpose.

7. Easy Spaghetti Carbonara

INGREDIENTS

- 1/4 cup of flour
- 1/4 cup of butter
- 1 liter of milk
- 1/8 teaspoon of pepper
- 1/2 teaspoon of salt
- 18 oz. bacon sliced extra thick
- 1/4 cup of olive oil
- 12 oz. sliced mushrooms
- 6-tablespoons of chopped shallots
- Cook 1-pound of spaghetti according to the package insert
- 2-teaspoons finely chopped parsley
- 1/2 cup of grated Parmesan cheese

- 2-ounces of freshly grated Fontina cheese

DIRECTIONS

1. Melt butter over medium heat in a 4-quart casserole.

2. Remove the meal and prepare dinner for 1 minute. Add milk, pepper, and pepper, and start with a wire beater until the mixture boils slightly. Reduce the heat and cook for 5 minutes, even if the sauce thickens. Stir the Fontina cheese into the sauce and let it soften in the sauce. Stay warm.

3. Prepare the bacon thoroughly for dinner. Drain on paper towels. Cut into 1/4-inch pieces and whisk in the sauce. In a large skillet, soften the olive oil over medium heat. Attach sliced onions and chopped mushrooms and fry until golden brown; adhere to the sauce. Cook spaghetti in the direction of the box. Drain well and add the parsley to the sauce. Mix well and move to a serving table. Sprinkle with Parmesan cheese and let it function as quickly as possible.

8. Oriental Apple Bee Salad

Prep time 10 min serves: 2

INGREDIENTS

- 1 lb. skinless chicken breast 2-servings
- 2-tablespoons of olive oil
- 1/2 teaspoon of salt
- 1/4 teaspoon black pepper
- 1/2 cup of sliced almonds
- 8-cups of romaine lettuce
- 1/4 cup sliced carrots
- 1/2 cup of crispy rice noodles
- 4-tablespoons Applebee's Oriental Salad Dressing

DIRECTIONS

1. Heat the grill to medium, or heat a sturdy iron skillet or grill pan over medium heat. Place the hand between two 'plastic wrap' and lift them to 3/8 min. Fizzy with the other oil and top with some pepper and pepper.

2. Grill them for 5 to 7 minutes on each side, until cooked through. Place them on a plate for four to five minutes rather than sliced to relax.

3. Roast the almonds in a little dry sauce over the heat of it

4. Supervise them - there is a high-quality line between toasted almonds and burnt almonds! Shake the pan gently when you start to smell the almonds, toast for a few more seconds, and immediately put the almonds on a paper towel. Let them cool down or.

5. Like salads, by putting down the lettuce first, 3 to 4 choices start with the food.

6. Sprinkle each with 2-tablespoons of carrots, 1/4 cup of crispy rice noodles, and 1/4 cup of toasted almonds. Place the poultry on top. Serve with loads of the Applebee's Oriental Salad Dressing.

9. Chorizo & Grits Breakfast Bowls

Total Time Prep/Total Time: 30 min. Makes 6 servings

INGREDIENTS

- 2 teaspoons olive oil
- 1 bundle (12 ounces) completely cooked chorizo chicken frankfurters or kind of decision, cut
- 1 enormous zucchini, chopped
- 3 cups water
- 3/4 cup speedy cooking corn meal
- 1 can (15 ounces) dark beans, flushed and depleted
- 1/2 cup shredded cheddar

- 6 enormous eggs
- Optional: Pico de Gallo and chopped new cilantro

DIRECTIONS

1. In an enormous skillet, heat oil over medium heat. Add hotdog; cook and mix until delicately browned, 2-3 minutes. Add zucchini; cook and mix until delicate, 4-5 minutes longer. Eliminate from pan; keep warm.

2. Then, in an enormous saucepan, heat water to the point of boiling. Gradually mix in corn meal. Decrease heat to medium-low; cook, covered, until thickened, blending occasionally, around 5 minutes. Mix in beans and cheddar until mixed. Eliminate from heat.

3. Wipe skillet clean; cover with cooking shower and spot over medium heat. In clusters, break 1 egg at an at once. Promptly lessen heat to low; cook until whites are totally set and yolks start to thicken yet are not hard, around 5 minutes.

4. To serve, partition corn meal blend among 6 dishes. Top with chorizo combination, eggs and, whenever wanted, Pico de Gallo and cilantro.

10. Simple Poached Salmon

Total Time Prep: 10 min. Cook: 1-1/2 hours Makes 4 servings

INGREDIENTS

- 2 cups water
- 1 cup white wine
- 1 medium onion, sliced
- 1 celery rib, slashed
- 1 medium carrot, sliced
- 2 tablespoons lemon juice
- 3 thyme sprigs
- 1 fresh rosemary sprig
- 1 bay leaf
- 1/2 teaspoon salt
- 1/4 teaspoon pepper

- 4 salmon fillets (1-1/4 inches thick and 6 ounces each)
- Lemon wedges

DIRECTIONS

1. Firstly In a 3-qt. slow cooker combines the first 11 INGREDIENTS. Cook, covered, on low 45 minutes.
2. Carefully place fillets in liquid; add additional warm water (120° to 130°) to cover if needed. Cook, covered, just until fish flakes easily with a fork (a thermometer inserted in fish should read at least 145°), 45-55 minutes. Then Remove fish from cooking liquid. And Serve warm or cold with lemon wedges.

11. Apple Balsamic Chicken

Total Time Prep: 15 min. Cook: 4 hours Makes 4 servings

INGREDIENTS

- 4 bone-in chicken thighs (around 1-1/2 pounds), skin eliminated
- 1/2 cup chicken stock
- 1/4 cup apple juice or juice
- 1/4 cup balsamic vinegar
- 2 tablespoons lemon juice
- 1/2 teaspoon salt
- 1/2 teaspoon garlic powder
- 1/2 teaspoon dried thyme
- 1/2 teaspoon paprika
- 1/2 teaspoon pepper
- 2 tablespoons spread

- 2 tablespoons generally useful flour

DIRECTIONS

1. Spot chicken in a 1-1/2-qt. slow cooker. In a little bowl, consolidate the stock, juice, vinegar, lemon juice and flavors; pour over meat. Cover and cook on low for 4-5 hours or until chicken is delicate.

2. Eliminate chicken; keep warm. Skim fat from cooking fluid. In a little pot, liquefy margarine; mix in flour until smooth. Steadily add cooking fluid. Heat to the point of boiling; cook and mix for 2-3 minutes or until thickened. Present with chicken.

12. Sausage-Stuffed Flank Steak

Total Time Prep: 35 min. Cook: 6 hours Makes 2 servings

INGREDIENTS

- 1/4 cup dried cherries
- 3/4 cup dry red wine or meat stock, separated
- 1 meat flank steak (1-1/2 pounds)
- 3/4 teaspoon salt, separated
- 1/2 teaspoon pepper, separated
- 1 medium onion, finely chopped
- 3 tablespoons olive oil, partitioned
- 4 garlic cloves, minced
- 1/2 cup prepared bread pieces
- 1/4 cup pitted Greek olives, split
- 1/4 cup ground Parmesan cheddar

- 1/4 cup minced new basil
- 1/2 pound mass hot Italian hotdog
- 1 container (24 ounces) marinara sauce
- Hot cooked pasta

DIRECTIONS

1. In a little bowl, join cherries and 1/4 cup wine; let stand 10 minutes. In the mean time, cut steak into four serving-size pieces; level to 1/4-in. thickness. Sprinkle the two sides with 1/2 teaspoon salt and 1/4 teaspoon pepper.

2. In a huge skillet, sauté onion in 1 tablespoon oil until delicate. Add garlic; cook brief longer. Move to an enormous bowl; mix in bread scraps, olives, cheddar, basil, cherry blend and staying salt and pepper. Disintegrate frankfurter over combination and blend well.

3. Spread 1/2 cup hotdog combination over every steak piece. Move up jam move style, beginning with a long side; attach with kitchen string.

4. In a similar skillet, earthy colored meat in leftover oil on all sides. Move to a lubed 3-qt. slow cooker. Top with marinara sauce and

remaining wine. Cook and cook on low for 6-8 hours or until meat is delicate. Present with pasta.

13. Pork with Peach Picante Sauce

Total Time Prep: 20 min. + chilling Cook: 5-1/2 hours Makes 4 servings

INGREDIENTS

- 2 pounds boneless country-style pork ribs
- 2 tablespoons taco seasoning
- 1/2 cup mild salsa
- 1/4 cup peach preserves
- 1/4 cup barbecue sauce
- 2 cups chopped fresh peeled peaches sour sliced peaches, thawed and chopped

DIRECTIONS

1. Firstly In a large bowl, toss ribs with taco seasoning. Cover and refrigerate overnight.

2. Place pork in a 3-qt. slow cooker. In a little bowl, combine the salsa, preserves and barbecue sauce. Pour over ribs. Then Cover and cook on low for 5-6 hours or until meat is tender.

3. Add peaches; cover and cook 30 minutes longer or until peaches are tender.

14. Chicken & Vegetables with Mustard-Herb Sauce

Total Time Prep: 20 min. Cook: 6 hours Makes 4 servings

INGREDIENTS

- 4 medium red potatoes, quartered
- 3 medium parsnips, cut into 1-inch pieces
- 2 medium leeks (white portion only), thinly slashed
- 3/4 cup fresh baby carrots
- 4 chicken leg quarters, skin removed
- 1 can (10-3/4 ounces) condensed cream of chicken soup with herbs, undiluted
- 2 tablespoons minced fresh parsley
- 1 tablespoon new dill or 1 teaspoon dill weed
- 1 tablespoon mustard

DIRECTIONS

1. Then In a 5- or 6-qt. slow cooker, place the potatoes, parsnips, leeks, carrots and chicken; pour soup over top. Cover and cook on low for 6-8 hours or until chicken is tender.

2. Then Remove chicken and vegetables; cover it and keep warm. Stir the parsley, dill and mustard into cooking juices; present with chicken and vegetables.

15. Peppery Chicken with Potatoes

Total Time Prep: 20 min. Cook: 5 hours + standing

Makes 4 servings

INGREDIENTS

- 1 pound red potatoes (around 6 medium), cut into wedges
- 1 huge onion, chopped
- 2 teaspoons salt
- 1 teaspoon paprika
- 1/2 teaspoon onion powder
- 1/2 teaspoon garlic powder
- 1/2 teaspoon dried thyme
- 1/2 teaspoon white pepper
- 1/2 teaspoon cayenne pepper
- 1/4 teaspoon pepper
- 1 oven/fryer chicken (3-1/2 to 4 pounds)

DIRECTIONS

1. Spot potatoes and onion in a 6-qt. slow cooker. In a little bowl, blend flavors. Fold wings under chicken; integrate drumsticks. Rub preparing combination over outside and within chicken. Spot chicken over vegetables.

2. Cook, covered, on low 5-6 hours or until a thermometer embedded in thickest piece of thigh peruses 170°-175°. Eliminate chicken from slow cooker; tent with foil. Let stand 15 minutes prior to cutting.

3. Move vegetables to a platter; keep warm. Whenever wanted, skim fat and thicken cooking juices for sauce. Present with chicken.

16. Chicken Tagine with Pumpkin

Total Time Prep: 35 min. Cook: 5 hours Makes 4 servings

INGREDIENTS

- 1 pound boneless skinless chicken thighs, cut into 1/2-inch pieces
- 1 can (15 ounces) garbanzo beans or chickpeas, flushed and depleted
- 1 can (14-1/2 ounces) diced tomatoes, undrained
- 1 medium green pepper, chopped
- 1 cup canned pumpkin
- 1/4 cup brilliant raisins
- 1 tablespoon maple syrup
- 2 teaspoons ground cumin
- 1 teaspoon ground cinnamon

- 1/2 teaspoon salt
- 1/2 teaspoon ground coriander
- 1/4 teaspoon cayenne pepper
- 1/4 teaspoon ground cloves
- 1/4 teaspoon ground allspice
- 1 tablespoon olive oil
- 1 medium onion, chopped
- 2 garlic cloves, minced
- 1 teaspoon minced new gingerroot
- Hot cooked couscous and chopped new cilantro

DIRECTIONS

1. In a 3-or 4-qt. slow cooker, join the initial 14 INGREDIENTS. In a little skillet, heat oil over medium heat. Add onion; cook and mix until delicate, 5-7 minutes. Add garlic and ginger; cook brief longer. Mix into slow cooker.

2. Cook, covered, on low until chicken is cooked through and vegetables are delicate, 5-6 hours. Present with couscous; sprinkle with cilantro.

17. Mexican Beef-Stuffed Peppers

Total Time Prep: 15 min. Cook: 5 hours Makes 4

servings

INGREDIENTS

- 4 medium green or sweet red peppers
- 1 pound ground hamburger
- 1 bundle (8.8 ounces) prepared to-serve Spanish rice
- 2 cups destroyed Colby-Monterey Jack cheddar, isolated
- 1-1/2 cups salsa
- 1 tablespoon hot pepper sauce
- 1 cup water
- 2 tablespoons minced new cilantro

DIRECTIONS

1. Cut tops off peppers and eliminate seeds; put in a safe spot. In an enormous skillet, cook meat over medium heat until not, at this point pink; channel.

2. Mix in the rice, 1-1/2 cups cheddar, salsa and pepper sauce. Spoon into peppers. Move to a 5-qt. slow cooker. Pour water around peppers.

3. Cover and cook on low for 5-6 hours or until peppers are delicate and filling is heated through. Top with residual cheddar; sprinkle with cilantro.

18. Easy Lamb kleftiko

5 Hours + Marinating Serves 4

INGREDIENTS

- lemon 1 enormous, squeezed
- extra-virgin olive oil 100ml
- dry white wine 175ml
- Dark peppercorns squashed to make ½ tsp.
- garlic 4 cloves, stripped and left entirety
- Dried oregano 2 tsp.
- Ground cumin 1 tsp.
- sheep shanks 4
- Ocean salt drops 1 tsp.
- ready tomato 1 enormous, cut into quarters
- cinnamon stick 1
- waxy potatoes 750g, stripped and cut into reduced down 3D squares
- level leaf parsley a modest bunch, generally chopped

DIRECTIONS:

1. Put the lemon juice, 2 tbsp. oil, wine, pepper, garlic, oregano and cumin into a blender and whizz. Put the shanks into a bowl, pour over the marinade and back rub well to cover. Cover and chill for at any rate 1 hour yet ideally overnight.

2. Heat the slow cooker to high or low, contingent upon wanted cooking time.

3. Put the meat, marinade, salt, tomato and cinnamon stick into the slow cooker. Cover with the top and cook for 3-4 hours on high, or 6-8 hours on low until totally delicate.

4. At the point when the sheep is cooked through and totally delicate, earthy colored the potatoes in 3 tbsp. of olive oil in a griddle over a medium-high heat until they start to shading and relax.

5. Eliminate the sheep from the slow cooker, put on a plate and cover firmly with foil.

6. Add the seared potatoes to the slow cooker and blend well. Cover and keep cooking for an additional 45 minutes-1 hour or until the potatoes are cooked and delicate. Add the sheep back to the slow cooker to heat through

again. Check the flavoring, adding more if vital.

7. Present with hard bread and a green serving of mixed greens.

19. Delicious Chicken Curry

Total Time Prep: 20 min. Cook: 4-1/2 hours Makes 4 servings

INGREDIENTS

- 4 bone-in chicken bosom parts, skin eliminated (8 ounces each)
- 1 can (15 ounces) cannellini beans, flushed and depleted
- 3/4 cup meagerly cut sweet onion
- 1/2 cup chopped sweet red pepper
- 1 cup peach salsa
- 1 tablespoon curry powder
- 1/2 teaspoon salt
- 1/4 teaspoon pepper
- 1 cup new green beans, managed and cut down the middle

- 2 tablespoons cornstarch
- 1/2 cup cold water
- 1-1/2 cups chicken stock
- 1-1/2 cups uncooked moment rice

DIRECTIONS

1. Spot the chicken, cannellini beans, onion and red pepper in 4-qt. slow cooker. In a little bowl, join the salsa, curry powder, salt and pepper; pour up and over.

2. Cover and cook on low for 4-5 hours or until chicken is delicate. Mix in green beans. Join cornstarch and water until smooth; continuously mix into slow cooker. Cover and cook on high for 30 minutes or until sauce is thickened.

3. In a huge pot, heat stock to the point of boiling; mix in rice. Cover and eliminate from the heat. Let represent 5 minutes or until fluid is consumed and rice is delicate. Cushion with a fork. Present with chicken and sauce.

20. Waffle Monte Cristos

Total Time Prep/Total Time: 20 min. Makes 4 servings

INGREDIENTS

- 1/2 cup apricot jam
- 8 frozen waffles
- 4 cuts store turkey
- 4 cuts shop ham
- 4 cuts Havarti cheddar (around 3 ounces)
- 4 bacon strips, cooked
- 2 tablespoons margarine, relaxed
- Maple syrup

DIRECTIONS

1. Preheat frying pan over medium heat. Spread jelly more than four waffles. Layer with turkey, ham, cheddar and bacon; top with outstanding waffles. Softly spread exterior of waffles with margarine.

2. Spot on frying pan; cook 4-5 minutes on each side or until brilliant brown and heated through. Present with syrup for plunging.

3. Wellbeing Tip: Yep, this is one debauched sandwich. Use cooking splash rather than spread and cut the bacon and cheddar down the middle to save 130 calories, 7 g immersed fat and very nearly 300 mg sodium for every serving.

21. Spicy Mongolian Beef Salad

Total Time Prep/Total Time: 30 min. Makes 4 servings

INGREDIENTS

- 1/4 cup olive oil
- 2 tablespoons rice vinegar
- 1 tablespoon reduced-sodium soy sauce
- 1 tablespoon sesame oil
- 2 teaspoons minced fresh gingerroot
- 1 small garlic clove, minced
- 1 teaspoon sugar
- BEEF:
- 1 tablespoon reduced-sodium soy sauce
- 2 garlic cloves, minced

- 2 teaspoons sugar
- 1 to 2 teaspoons crushed red pepper flakes
- 1 teaspoon sesame oil
- 1 beef top sirloin steak (1 pound), cut into 1/4-inch strips
- 1 tablespoon olive oil
- SALAD:
- 8 cups torn mixed salad greens
- 1 cup shredded carrots
- 1/2 cup thinly sliced cucumber
- 4 radishes, thinly sliced

DIRECTIONS

1. Whisk together first 7 INGREDIENTS.
2. Combine first 5 beef INGREDIENTS; toss with beef strips. In a large cast-iron or other heavy skillet, heat olive oil over medium-high heat; stir-fry beef mixture until browned, 2-3 minutes. Remove from pan.
3. Combine salad INGREDIENTS; divide among 4 plates. Top with beef. Drizzle with dressing.

22. Spinach-Artichoke Rigatoni

Total Time Prep/Total Time: 30 min. Makes 4 servings

INGREDIENTS

- 3 cups uncooked rigatoni or huge tube pasta
- 1 bundle (10 ounces) frozen creamed spinach
- 1 can (14 ounces) water-stuffed artichoke hearts, washed, depleted and quartered
- 2 cups shredded part-skim mozzarella cheddar, isolated
- 1/4 cup ground Parmesan cheddar
- 1/2 teaspoon salt
- 1/4 teaspoon pepper

DIRECTIONS

1. Preheat grill. Get ready rigatoni and spinach as per bundle DIRECTIONS.

2. Channel pasta, saving 1/2 cup pasta water; get back to pan. Add artichoke hearts, 1/2 cup mozzarella cheddar, Parmesan cheddar, salt, pepper and creamed spinach; throw to join, adding a portion of the held pasta water to thin, whenever wanted.

3. Move to a lubed 2-qt. grill safe preparing dish; sprinkle with residual mozzarella cheddar. Sear 4-6 in. from heat 2-3 minutes or until cheddar is dissolved.

23. Easy Stuffed Peppers recipe

Total Time Prep: 15 min. Cook: 3 hours Makes 4 servings

INGREDIENTS:

- 1/2 cup frozen corn
- 1/3 cup uncooked converted long grain rice
- 1-1/4 teaspoons chili powder
- 1/2 teaspoon ground cumin
- Reduced-fat sour cream, optional
- 4 medium sweet red peppers
- 1 can (15 ounces) black beans, rinsed and drained
- 1 cup shredded pepper jack cheese
- 3/4 cup salsa
- 1 small onion, chopped

DIRECTIONS

1. Firstly Cut and discard tops from peppers; remove seeds. In a large bowl, mix beans, cheese, salsa, onion, corn, rice, chili powder and cumin; spoon into peppers. Place in a 5-qt. slow cooker coated with cooking spray.

2. Then Cook, covered, on low until peppers are tender and filling is heated through, 3-4 hours. If desired, serve with sour cream.

24. Tangy Pulled Pork Sandwiches

Total Time Prep: 10 min. Cook: 4 hours Makes 4 servings

INGREDIENTS

- 1 pork tenderloin (1 pound)
- 1 cup ketchup
- 2 tablespoons plus 1-1/2 teaspoons brown sugar
- 2 tablespoons plus 1-1/2 teaspoons cider vinegar
- 1 tablespoon plus 1-1/2 teaspoons Worcestershire sauce
- 1 tablespoon spicy brown mustard
- 1/4 teaspoon pepper
- 4 rolls or buns, split and toasted
- Coleslaw, optional

DIRECTIONS

1. Firstly Cut the tenderloin in half; place in a 3-qt. slow cooker. Combine the ketchup, brown sugar, vinegar, Worcestershire sauce, mustard and pepper; pour over pork.

2. Then Cover and cook on low for 4-5 hours or until meat is tender. Remove meat; shred with 2 forks. Now return to slow cooker; heat through. Serve on toasted rolls or buns, with coleslaw if desired.

25. Easy Ribs Dinner

Total Time Prep: 10 min. Cook: 6-1/4 hours Makes 4 servings

INGREDIENTS

- 2 pounds boneless country-style pork ribs
- 1/2 teaspoon salt
- 1/4 teaspoon pepper
- 8 small red potatoes (about 1 pound), halved
- 4 medium carrots, cut into 1-inch pieces
- 3 celery ribs, cut into 1/2-inch pieces
- 1 medium onion, coarsely chopped
- 3/4 cup water
- 1 garlic clove, crushed
- 1 can (10-3/4 ounces) condensed cream mushroom soup, undiluted

DIRECTIONS

1. Firstly Sprinkle ribs with salt and pepper; transfer to a 4-qt. slow cooker. Add potatoes, carrots, celery, onion, water and garlic. Cook, covered, on low until meat and vegetables are tender, 6-8 hours.

2. Then Remove meat and vegetables; skim fat from cooking juices. Whisk soup into cooking juices; return meat and vegetables to slow cooker. Cook, covered until heated through, 15-30 minutes longer.

26. Creamy Italian Chicken

Total Time Prep: 15 min. Cook: 4 hours Makes 4 servings

INGREDIENTS

- 4 boneless skinless chicken breast parts (6 ounces each)
- 1 envelope Italian plate of mixed greens dressing blend
- 1/4 cup water
- 1 bundle (8 ounces) cream cheddar, mollified
- 1 can (10-3/4 ounces) consolidated cream of chicken soup, undiluted
- 1 can (4 ounces) mushroom stems and pieces, depleted
- Hot cooked pasta or rice
- Minced new oregano, discretionary

DIRECTIONS

1. Spot the chicken in a 3-qt. slow cooker. Consolidate serving of mixed greens dressing blend and water; pour over chicken. Cover and cook on low for 3 hours. Eliminate chicken. Cool marginally; shred meat with two forks. Get back to slow cooker.

2. In a little bowl, beat cream cheddar and soup until mixed. Mix in mushrooms. Pour over chicken. Cover and cook until chicken is delicate, 1 hour longer. Present with pasta or rice. Whenever wanted, sprinkle with oregano.

27. Easy Chutney-Glazed Carrots

Total Time Prep: 15 min. Cook: 4 hours Makes 4 servings

INGREDIENTS

- 1/3 cup mango chutney
- 2 tablespoons sugar
- 2 tablespoons minced new parsley
- 2 tablespoons white wine or unsweetened squeezed apple
- 1 tablespoon Dijon mustard
- 1 tablespoon spread, liquefied
- 1 garlic clove, minced
- 1/2 teaspoon salt
- 1/4 teaspoon ground ginger
- 1/4 teaspoon pepper

- 1 pound new carrots, cut into 1/4-inch cuts (around 4 cups)

DIRECTIONS

1. Spot the initial 10 INGREDIENTS in a 3-qt. slow cooker. Add carrots; throw to join.
2. Cook, covered, on low 4-5 hours or until carrots are delicate. Mix prior to serving.

28. Simmered Turkey Enchiladas

Total Time Prep: 10 min. Cook: 6 hours Makes 4 servings

INGREDIENTS

- 2 pounds turkey thighs or drumsticks
- 1 can (8 ounces) pureed tomatoes
- 1 can (4 ounces) slashed green chilies
- 1/3 cup slashed onion
- 2 tablespoons Worcestershire sauce
- 1 to 2 tablespoons bean stew powder
- 1/4 teaspoon garlic powder
- 8 flour tortillas (6 inches), warmed
- Discretionary fixings: Chopped green onions, cut ready olives, slashed tomatoes, destroyed cheddar, harsh cream and destroyed lettuce

DIRECTIONS

1. Eliminate skin from turkey; place turkey in a 5-qt. slow cooker. In a little bowl, consolidate the pureed tomatoes, chilies, onion, Worcestershire sauce, bean stew powder and garlic powder; pour over turkey. Cover and cook on low until turkey is delicate, 6-8 hours.

2. Eliminate turkey; shred meat with a fork and get back to the slow cooker. Heat through.

3. Spoon around 1/2 cup turkey combination down the focal point of every tortilla. Overlay lower part of tortilla over topping and move off. Add fixings of your decision.

4. Freeze choice: Individually wrap cooled burritos in paper towels and foil; freeze in a cooler compartment. To utilize, eliminate foil; place paper towel-wrapped burrito on a microwave-safe plate. Microwave on high until heated through, 3-4 minutes, turning once. Let stand 20 seconds.

29. Easy Home-Style Chicken Soup

Total Time Prep: 15 min. Cook: 6-1/4 hours Makes 4 servings

INGREDIENTS

- 1 can (14-1/2 ounces) reduced-sodium chicken broth
- 1 can (14-1/2 ounces) diced tomatoes, undrained
- 1 cup cubed cooked chicken
- 1 can (8 ounces) mushroom stems and pieces, drained
- 1/4 cup sliced fresh carrot
- 1/4 cup sliced celery
- 1 bay leaf
- 1/8 teaspoon dried thyme
- 3/4 cup uncooked egg noodles

DIRECTIONS

1. In a 1-1/2-qt. slow cooker, combine the first eight INGREDIENTS. Cover and cook on low for 6 hours. Stir in noodles; cover and cook on high for 15-20 minutes or until tender. Discard bay leaf.

30. Slow & Easy Baby Back Ribs

Total Time Prep: 20 min. Cook: 5 hours Makes 4 servings

INGREDIENTS

- 4 pounds pork infant back ribs, cut into 2-rib partitions
- 1 medium onion, cleaved
- 1/2 cup ketchup
- 1/4 cup pressed brown sugar
- 1/4 cup juice vinegar
- 1/4 cup tomato paste or pureed tomatoes
- 2 tablespoons paprika
- 2 tablespoons Worcestershire sauce
- 1 tablespoon arranged mustard
- 1 teaspoon salt
- 1/4 teaspoon pepper

- 2 tablespoons cornstarch
- 2 tablespoons cold water

DIRECTIONS

1. Spot ribs in a 5-qt. slow cooker. In a little bowl, join the onion, ketchup, earthy colored sugar, vinegar, tomato paste, paprika, Worcestershire, mustard, salt and pepper; pour over ribs. Cover and cook on low for 5-6 hours or until meat is delicate.

2. Eliminate ribs to a serving platter; keep warm. Skim fat from cooking juices; move juices to a little pot. Heat to the point of boiling.

3. Consolidate cornstarch and water until smooth. Step by step mix into the skillet. Heat to the point of boiling; cook and mix for 2 minutes or until thickened. Present with ribs.

31. Tropical Pork Chops

Total Time Prep: 15 min. Cook: 3 hours Makes 4 servings

INGREDIENTS

- 2 containers (23-1/2 ounces each) blended tropical natural product, depleted and slashed
- 3/4 cup defrosted limeade concentrate
- 1/4 cup sweet bean stew sauce
- 1 garlic clove, minced
- 1 teaspoon minced new gingerroot
- 4 bone-in pork flank cleaves (3/4 inch thick and 5 ounces each)
- 1 green onion, finely slashed
- 2 tablespoons minced new cilantro
- 2 tablespoons minced new mint
- 2 tablespoons fragmented almonds, toasted

- 2 tablespoons finely slashed solidified ginger, discretionary
- 1/2 teaspoon ground lime zing

DIRECTIONS

1. In a 3-qt. slow cooker, join the initial 5 INGREDIENTS. Add pork, masterminding cleaves to sit cozily in organic product blend. Cook, covered, on low until meat is delicate (a thermometer embedded in pork should peruse at any rate 145°), 3-4 hours.

2. In a little bowl, blend remaining INGREDIENTS. To serve, eliminate pork cleaves from slow cooker. Using an opened spoon, serve organic product over pork. Sprinkle with spice blend.

32. Sweet Onion & Cherry Pork Chops

Total Time Prep: 15 min. Cook: 3 hours Makes 2 servings

INGREDIENTS

- 1/2 cup fresh or frozen pitted tart cherries, thawed
- 2 tablespoons chopped sweet onion
- 1 tablespoon honey
- 1/2 teaspoon seasoned salt
- 1/4 teaspoon pepper
- 2 boneless pork loin chops (5 ounces each)
- 1 teaspoon cornstarch
- 1 teaspoon cold water

DIRECTIONS

1. Firstly In a 1-1/2-qt. slow cooker, combine the first 5 INGREDIENTS; top with pork chops. Cover and cook on low until meat is tender, 3-4 hours.

2. Remove meat to a serving platter; keep warm. Skim fat from cooking juices; transfer to a small saucepan. Then bring liquid to a boil. Combine cornstarch and water until smooth. Gradually stir into the pan. Bring to a boil; cook and stir until thickened, about 2 minutes. Serve with meat.

33. Goat Cheese & Ham Omelet

Total Time Prep/Total Time: 20 min. Makes 1 serving

INGREDIENTS

- 4 huge egg whites
- 2 teaspoons water
- 1/8 teaspoon pepper
- 1 cut shop ham, finely chopped
- 2 tablespoons finely chopped green pepper
- 2 tablespoons finely chopped onion
- 2 tablespoons disintegrated goat cheddar
- Minced new parsley, optional

DIRECTIONS

1. In a small bowl, whisk egg whites, water and pepper until mixed; mix in ham, green pepper and onion. Heat a huge nonstick skillet covered with cooking splash over medium-high heat. Pour in egg white combination. Blend should set quickly at edges. As egg whites set, push cooked segments toward the middle, allowing uncooked egg to stream under.

2. At the point when no fluid egg remains, sprinkle goat cheddar on 1 side. Overlap omelet fifty-fifty; slide onto a plate. Whenever wanted, sprinkle with parsley.

34. Orange-Glazed Pork with Sweet Potatoes

Total Time Prep: 20 min. Bake: 55 min. + standing

Makes 6 servings

INGREDIENTS

- 1 pound yams (around 2 medium)
- 2 medium apples
- 1 medium orange
- 1 teaspoon salt
- 1/2 teaspoon pepper
- 1 cup squeezed orange
- 2 tablespoons brown sugar
- 2 teaspoons cornstarch
- 1 teaspoon ground cinnamon
- 1 teaspoon ground ginger
- 2 pork tenderloins (around 1 pound each)

DIRECTIONS

1. Preheat oven to 350°. Strip yams; center apples. Cut potatoes, apples and orange transversely into 1/4-in. - thick cuts. Organize in a foil-lined 15x10x1-in. heating container covered with cooking shower; sprinkle with salt and pepper. Cook 10 minutes.

2. Then, in a microwave-safe bowl, blend squeezed orange, brown sugar, cornstarch, cinnamon and ginger. Microwave, covered, on high, mixing like clockwork until thickened, 1-2 minutes. Mix until smooth.

3. Spot pork over yam combination; sprinkle with squeezed orange blend. Broil until a thermometer embedded in pork peruses 145° and yams and apples are delicate, 45-55 minutes longer. Eliminate from oven; tent with foil. Let stand 10 minutes prior to cutting.

35. Salmon Veggie Packets

Total Time Prep/Total Time: 30 min. Makes 4 servings

INGREDIENTS

- 2 tablespoons white wine
- 1 tablespoon olive oil
- 1/4 teaspoon salt
- 1/4 teaspoon pepper
- 2 medium sweet yellow peppers, julienned
- 2 cups new sugar snap peas, managed
- SALMON:
- 2 tablespoons white wine
- 1 tablespoon olive oil
- 1 tablespoon ground lemon zing
- 1/2 teaspoon salt

- 1/4 teaspoon pepper
- 4 salmon filets (6 ounces each)
- 1 medium lemon, split

DIRECTIONS

1. Preheat oven to 400°. Cut four 18x15-in. bits of material paper or uncompromising foil: overlay each transversely down the middle, shaping a wrinkle. In a huge bowl, blend wine, oil, salt and pepper. Add vegetables and throw to cover.

2. In a small bowl, blend the initial five salmon INGREDIENTS. To collect, expose one piece of material paper; place a salmon filet on one side. Sprinkle with 2 teaspoons wine combination; top with one-fourth of the vegetables.

3. Overlay paper over fish and vegetables; overlap the open closures multiple times to seal. Rehash with outstanding parcels. Spot on heating sheets.

4. Heat until fish simply starts to chip effectively with a fork, 12-16 minutes, and opening parcels cautiously to allow steam to get away.

5. To serve, press lemon juice over vegetables.

36. Easy protein Lamb meal

Prep Time 15 mins Cook Time 30 mins Total Time 45 mins

INGREDIENTS

- 2 ½ pounds lamb shoulder chops, see note below
- 1 large sweet potato
- 8 red new potatoes
- 2 Tablespoons olive oil
- 2 Tablespoons chopped fresh rosemary
- 1 Tablespoon chopped fresh thyme leaves
- Salt and freshly ground pepper
- 2 large garlic cloves, sliced
- 1 pint grape or cherry tomatoes

- 8 ounces frozen green peas

DIRECTIONS:

1. Preheat oven to 400°F.
2. Trim the enormous bits of fat from the sheep and cut into 2-inch lumps.
3. Strip the yam and the new potatoes and cut into 2-inch lumps.
4. On an enormous rimmed sheet dish (12x17), throw the sheep and the potatoes with the olive oil, at that point sprinkle the spices overall and throw until equitably covered.
5. Add salt and pepper as you would prefer and throw. (At the point when I make this for my more distant family I leave it off by and large and let everybody add their own. My significant other loves salt and pepper, so when it's simply us, I use it liberally.)
6. Spread the meat and vegetables out on the plate equitably and dissipate the cut garlic on top.
7. Slide this into your preheated oven and meal for 20 minutes, throwing part of the way through cooking. Meat ought to be browned.

(We like our sheep cooked medium-well. Assuming you need your meat more uncommon, start the potatoes and add the meat 5 to 10 minutes after the fact.)

8. Add the tomatoes and the peas to the sheet skillet and cook for an extra 10 minutes.

9. The store where I purchase my meat had 2 kinds of shoulder slashes, sharp edge and round bone. You need the hacks with the round bone; they are simpler to work with. Likewise, you can request that your butcher 3D shape the meat for you to save time at home.

10. In the event that you don't care for sheep, have a go at subbing sirloin steak. You may require less, in light of the fact that sirloin is less greasy than sheep

37. High protein Wonton Soup

Prep Time: 1 HOUR Cook Time: 5 MINUTES Total Time: 1 HOUR 5 MINUTES Servings: 8 servings

INGREDIENTS

- 1 pack wonton coverings (80 coverings)
- Filling
- 1/2 lbs. (230 g) ground lean pork
- 1/2 lbs. (230 g) stripped shrimp, chopped into little pieces
- 1 tablespoon finely minced ginger
- 2 green onions , finely chopped
- 1 tablespoon light soy sauce (or soy sauce)
- 2 tablespoons Shaoxing wine (or dry sherry)
- 1/2 teaspoon salt
- 2 tablespoons sesame oil

- (Alternative 1) Chicken soup base
- 8 cups chicken stock
- 8 teaspoons light soy sauce (or soy sauce)
- 8 teaspoons minced ginger
- 8 teaspoons sesame oil
- Salt , to taste
- (Choice 2) Chinese road style soup base
- 8 cups hot stock from the wonton bubbling water
- 8 tablespoons papery dried shrimp , or to taste
- 8 major bits of dried ocean growth for soup , arranged by guidance (*Footnote 1)
- 4 teaspoons chicken bouillon
- 8 teaspoons light soy sauce , or to taste
- 8 teaspoons sesame oil
- Garnishes
- 4 green onions , chopped
- 4 stalks infant bok choy , slice to reduced down (or 4 cups infant spinach)
- 1 bunch cilantro, chopped (Optional)
- Hand crafted stew oil , to taste (Optional)

DIRECTIONS

1. Make the filling

2. Without a food processor: Combine ground pork, shrimp, ginger, green onion, soy sauce, Shaoxing wine, salt and sesame oil in a major bowl. Blend well in with a fork until everything consolidates well together and the combination feels somewhat tacky.

3. With a food processor or a blender: coarsely cleave the ginger and green onion. Add all the filling INGREDIENTS with the exception of the shrimp. Blend until it frames a velvety paste. Add the shrimp and mix once more, until the shrimp are finely chopped however don't turn into a paste.

4. Wrap the wonton

5. To make wontons, place a wonton covering in one hand, scoop a teaspoon of wonton filling and spot it close to the restricted side of the wonton covering (you can add more filling to the wonton on the off chance that you like, as long as you can in any case wrap it). Overlap the restricted side over the filling; at that point roll the filling right through the opposite side of the covering. Tie the two finishes and press

together to bolt the filling inside the covering. Brush a dainty layer of water onto the wonton covering and press the closures together.

6. Make each wonton in turn, and line up every one of the wontons on a major wooden cutting board. In the event that you're not going to heat up the wontons promptly, utilize a moist paper towel (or cheesecloth) to cover the wontons to keep them from drying out.

7. On the off chance that you're not going to heat up the wontons that very day, place them in a water/air proof holder with a few layers of wet paper towels on the base. Thusly, they can be put away in the cooler for as long as 2 days.

8. (Alternative 1) Make the chicken soup base

9. Consolidate the chicken stock, ginger, and soy sauce in a pot. Heat to the point of boiling. Let bubble for 10 minutes. Go to least heat to keep warm and begin cooking wontons (see beneath).

10. Plan 8 medium-sized dishes. Add the cooked wontons and bok choy. Add 2 tablespoons green onion, 1 tablespoon soy sauce and 1/2 teaspoon sesame oil into each bowl. Pour in 1

and 1/2 cups hot stock. Trimming with cilantro and stew oil, if using.

11. Serve hot.

12. (Alternative 2) Make the road seller style soup base

13. To get ready 1 serving of wonton soup base, add a major spoon of cilantro, 1 tablespoon papery dried shrimps, a liberal piece of dried kelp, 1/4 teaspoon chicken bouillon, and some child bok choy into a major bowl. Rehash the interaction to set up the remainder of the soup base in the other serving bowls. Cook wontons (see beneath).

14. To make 1 serving of wonton soup, utilize a spoon to move cooked wontons, bok choy, and the hot soup into a serving bowl with every one of the INGREDIENTS from the past advance. Sprinkle 1 teaspoon soy sauce and 1 teaspoon sesame oil into the bowl and give it a delicate mix. The soup ought to be golden hued. Add additional soy sauce or salt if the soup isn't sufficiently pungent. Dissipate green onion on top. Enhancement with cilantro and stew oil, if using.

15. Serve hot.

16. Heated up the wonton

17. To heat up the wontons, heat a major pot of water until bubbling. Add 10 to 20 wontons all at once and bubble over medium heat until wontons are drifting on the outside of the water. Keep on bubbling until the coverings are swollen, around 1 to 2 minutes for little wontons and 2 to 3 minutes for greater ones. Take a wonton out with an opened spoon and split it with a chopstick or fork. On the off chance that the wonton is cooked through, stop heat quickly and move the wontons to singular serving bowls. If not, keep on bubbling until cooked through.

18. Whenever you've cooked the wontons, add the bok choy. Let cook until delicate. Eliminate from the pot, channel well, and put in a safe spot.

19. To cook frozen wontons

20. Heat a huge pot of water to the point of boiling over high heat. Add wontons. Mix tenderly to keep from staying. Cook until heating the water to the point of boiling once more. Go to medium-low heat. Cover the pot with a little hole on one side, to forestall spilling. Keep

bubbling for 2 minutes (3 minutes for bigger wontons). Remain adjacent to the pot the entire chance to screen the stock. On the off chance that the stock begins to spill, reveal and mix, and supplant the cover. Uncover and keep cooking for one more moment, or until the wontons are cooked through.

21. There are numerous kinds of dried ocean growth. My unique formula utilized a sort of moment ocean growth that will rehydrate quickly once positioned into the hot soup. There are different kinds of fish that require some splashing prior to using. Peruse the rear of your bundle and adhere to the guidelines as needs be.

22. The sustenance realities for this formula are determined dependent on 1 bowl of chicken-stock based soup containing 10 wontons.

38. Easy Chicken And Shrimp

INGREDIENTS:

- Chicken and shrimp
- 2-tablespoons vegetable oil
- 1-chicken breast, cut into bite-sized pieces
- ¼ cup cornstarch
- 10-medium shrimp, peeled peanut sauce
- ¼ cup of creamy peanut butter
- 2-tablespoons water
- 1-tablespoon sugar
- 1-tablespoon reduced-sodium soy sauce
- 1-teaspoon rice vinegar
- 1-teaspoon lime juice
- ⅛ teaspoon red pepper flakes
- Curry coconut sauce
- 1-teaspoon olive oil

- 1-teaspoon sesame oil
- ⅛ teaspoon red pepper flakes
- 2-cloves garlic, finely chopped
- 1-small onion, chopped
- 1-teaspoon ginger, finely chopped
- ½ cup water
- ½ teaspoon ground cumin
- ½ teaspoon ground coriander
- 1-teaspoon paprika
- ¼ teaspoon salt (or to taste)
- ¼ teaspoon pepper (or to taste)
- ¼ teaspoon allspice
- ¼ teaspoon turmeric
- 1-can (14 ounces) of coconut milk
- 1-medium carrot, cut julienne
- 1-small zucchini, julienned
- ½ cup of frozen peas
- Garnish
- ½ cup coconut flakes, toasted
- ¼ cup peanuts, chopped
- 2-green onions, cut or chopped into julienne
- Sesame seeds (optional)
- 2-cups of rice, cooked

DIRECTIONS:

1. Heat the two tablespoons of oil in a large frying pan. Salt and pepper the chicken pieces to taste and dip them in the cornstarch. Do the same with the shrimp.

2. When the oil is hot, leave the chicken with it and cook until it starts to brown, about a few minutes. Then do the same with the shrimp, cook the shrimp until it just starts to turn pink.

3. Place the chicken and shrimp on a plate and set aside.

4. In a small saucepan, heat all the INGREDIENTS for the peanut sauce. Cook until just starting to boil, then remove from heat and set aside.

5. In another saucepan over medium heat, add 1-teaspoon of vegetable oil, vegetable oil, and ground red pepper flakes. Add the garlic, sliced onion, and ginger and cook until the onion is soft. Add the water and all the spices for the sauce and stir to mix. Bring this mixture to a boil. When it starts to boil, add the coconut milk and bring it back to a boil. Then reduce the heat and simmer for 20 minutes or until the sauce thickens nicely.

6. When the sauce has thickened, add the julienned carrots and zucchini and stir in the peas last—Cook for about 10 minutes more, or until the carrots are tender.

7. Before serving, place some rice on each plate and add some chicken and shrimp. Cover with the sauce and put some of the peanut sauce on top. Garnish with one or more of the above toppings under garnish.

39. Chicken with Broccoli and Sweet Potato Wedges

Prep time: 30 min Serves 4

INGREDIENTS

- 8 (3 1/2-oz.) chicken drumsticks, cleaned 1 tablespoon new lemon juice 1/8 teaspoons kosher salt, isolated 1/2 teaspoon poultry preparing 1 teaspoon garlic powder, separated 1/8 teaspoon newly ground dark pepper 2 huge eggs, gently thumped 1 cup panko (Japanese breadcrumbs) 1/2 ounces Parmesan cheddar, ground (around 1/3 cup) 1 teaspoon dried oregano 1 teaspoon dried parsley pieces (optional) Cooking splash 2 (7-oz.) yams, each cut into 8 wedges 2 tablespoons olive oil, partitioned 1/2 teaspoon paprika 1/2 teaspoon bean stew powder 7 cups broccoli florets (around 12 oz.) 1 garlic clove, squashed or ground 5 lemon wedges

DIRECTIONS:

1. Preheat oven to 425°F.

2. Spot chicken in an enormous bowl. Shower with lemon squeeze, and sprinkle with 3/8 teaspoon salt, poultry preparing, 1/2 teaspoon garlic powder, and dark pepper; throw to join.

3. Spot eggs in a shallow dish. Consolidate panko, Parmesan, oregano, and parsley, if using, in another shallow dish. Plunge every drumstick in eggs at that point dig in panko blend. Spot drumsticks on a rimmed heating sheet covered with cooking shower; dispose of outstanding egg and panko blend. Coat highest points of drumsticks with cooking splash. Prepare at 425°F for 15 minutes.

4. Consolidate potatoes, 1 tablespoon oil, staying 1/2 teaspoon garlic powder, paprika, bean stew powder, and 3/8 teaspoon salt; throw to

cover. Mastermind potatoes on one portion of another rimmed preparing sheet covered with cooking shower. Spot in oven with chicken, and heat at 425°F for 10 minutes.

5. Consolidate broccoli, staying 1 tablespoon oil, garlic clove, and staying 3/8 teaspoon salt. Eliminate heating sheet with potatoes from oven; turn potatoes over, and add broccoli to other portion of container. Spot in oven with chicken, and heat at 425°F for 20 minutes or until chicken and potatoes are finished. Crush 1 lemon wedge over broccoli. Serve remaining lemon wedges with the dinner.

40. Puff Pastry Chicken Bundles

Total Time Prep: 30 min. Bake: 20 min. Makes 8 servings

INGREDIENTS

- 8 boneless skinless chicken breast halves (about 6 ounces each)
- 1 teaspoon salt
- 1/2 teaspoon pepper
- 40 large spinach leaves
- 1 carton (8 ounces) spreadable chive and onion cream cheese
- 1/2 cup chopped walnuts, toasted
- 2 sheets frozen puff pastry, thawed
- 1 large egg
- 1/2 teaspoon cold water

DIRECTIONS

1. Preheat oven to 400°. Cut a longwise cut in every chicken bosom half to inside 1/2 in. of the opposite side; open meat so it lies level. Cover with cling wrap; pound with a meat mallet to 1/8-in. thickness. Eliminate plastic wrap. Sprinkle with salt and pepper.

2. Spot five spinach leaves on every chicken bosom half. Spoon a meager 2 tablespoons of cream cheddar down the focal point of every chicken bosom half; sprinkle with 1 tablespoon pecans. Move up chicken; wrap up closes.

3. Unfurl puff baked good; cut into eight segments. Fold each into a 7-in. square. Spot chicken on one portion of each square; overlay other portion of baked good over chicken. Pleat edges with fork. Consolidate egg and cold water; brush over edges of cake.

4. Heat on a lubed 15x10x1-in. heating sheet until a thermometer peruses 165°, 20-25 minutes.

41. 4 Easy Green Pepper Steak

Total Time Prep/Total Time: 30 min. Makes 4 servings

INGREDIENTS

- 1 tablespoon cornstarch
- 1/4 cup reduced-sodium soy sauce
- 1/4 cup water
- 2 tablespoons canola oil, divided
- 1 pound beef top sirloin steak, cut into 1/4-in.-thick strips
- 2 small onions, cut into thin wedges
- 2 celery ribs, sliced diagonally
- 1 medium green pepper, cut into 1-inch pieces
- 2 medium tomatoes, cut into wedges
- Hot cooked rice

DIRECTIONS

1. Combine cornstarch, soy sauce and water until smooth. In a large skillet, heat 1 tablespoon oil over medium-high heat; stir-fry beef until browned, 2-3 minutes. Remove from pan.

2. Stir-fry onions, celery and pepper in remaining oil 3 minutes. Stir cornstarch mixture; add to pan. Bring to a boil; cook and stir until thickened and bubbly, 1-2 minutes. Stir in tomatoes and beef; heat through. Present with rice.

42. Healthy Seafood Soup

22 MINUTES MIN 2 BOWLS SERVINGS

INGREDIENTS

- 2½ C vegetable stock
- 4 ocean scallops, washed and wiped off
- 2 C gluten free noodles, cooked as coordinated
- 1 carrot, stripped and julienned
- 2 celery ribs, meagerly cut
- 2 red radish, managed and daintily cut
- 1 C spring peas, shelled, pods disposed of
- 2 C shiitake mushroom covers, daintily cut
- 1 scallion, managed and daintily cut
- 2 cloves garlic, shredded
- 1 T new ginger, cleaned and shredded
- 1 T unsalted spread
- 1 T additional virgin olive oil

- 1 tsp. fit salt, more to taste
- run sriracha or other hot sauce
- embellish with sprinkling of miniature greens

DIRECTIONS

1. Wash and afterward strip, trim, cut hack, cut, dice or julienne vegetables as you wish. Wash ocean scallops and afterward wipe off.

2. Empty vegetable stock into a medium-sized pot. Heat to the point of boiling and afterward decrease to stew. Mix in garlic, ginger and salt. Cover.

3. Heat 5 cups of salted water to the point of boiling. Add dried noodles and cook as coordinated. Channel and gap into two soup bowls.

4. Simultaneously, carry a medium measured skillet to medium-high temperature. Add spread and olive oil, permitting them to mix and come to temperature. Add scallops, being mindful so as not to swarm them in the skillet. Burn one side, around 3-4 minutes, turn over and rehash. When cooked, eliminate from skillet and permit to rest.

5. Return stock to a bubble. Add vegetables and cook for 4 minutes.
6. Using an opened spoon, eliminate the entirety of the vegetables from the stock. Spoon onto cooked noodles, partitioning them uniformly between the two dishes.
7. Move two singed scallops into each bowl. Spoon equivalent measures of bubbling stock into each bowl.
8. Add a scramble of hot sauce to each bowl and trimming both with a sprinkling of micro-greens.

43. Beef Lettuce Cups with Carrot & Daikon Slaw

SERVINGS 4 PREP TIME 40 min COOK TIME 5 min

DURATION 45 min

INGREDIENTS

- 1/4 cup rice vinegar
- 1 tbsp. plus 1/2 tsp. raw honey, divided
- 1/8 tsp. sea salt
- 1 carrot, peeled and cut into matchsticks (1/cup)
- 1 daikon radish, cut into matchsticks (1/cup) (TIP: If you can't find daikon radish, regular radish works well here too.)
- 1 tsp. sesame oil
- 10 oz. lean ground beef

- 1/2 cup finely chopped red onion
- 3 cloves garlic, minced
- 1 tbsp. peeled and minced fresh ginger
- 1 1/3 cups BPA-free canned unsalted black beans, drained and rinsed
- 1 tbsp. reduced-sodium soy sauce
- 12 romaine lettuce leaves
- 2 tbsp. chopped roasted unsalted peanuts
- 2 tbsp. thinly sliced scallions

DIRECTIONS

1. Firstly In a medium bowl, whisk together vinegar, 1 tbsp. honey and salt. Add carrot and radish; toss to coat. Cover and transfer to refrigerator to marinate until tender and chilled, at least 2 hours or overnight.

2. Heat a large nonstick skillet on medium and brush with oil. Then Add beef and sauté until no longer pink, about 5 minutes. Push beef to one side of skillet. To other side, add onion, garlic and ginger; sauté until onion softens, about 2 minutes.

3. Add beans, soy sauce and remaining 1/2 tsp. honey and stir all INGREDIENTS together; simmer for 3 minutes, stirring occasionally.

4. Drain liquid from slaw. Fill in each lettuce leaf with 1/4 cup beef-bean mixture; top it with slaw. Garnish with peanuts and scallions.

44. Chicken enchilada bowl

Prep Time: 20 minutes Cook Time: 30 minutes Total Time: 50 minutes Yield: 4 servings

INGREDIENTS

- 2 tablespoons coconut oil (for singing chicken)
- 1 pound of boneless, skinless chicken thighs
- 3/4 cup red enchilada sauce (formula from Low Carb Maven)
- 1/4 cup water
- 1/4 cup chopped onion
- 1-4 oz. can diced green chilies
- Fixings (don't hesitate to modify)
- 1 entire avocado, diced
- 1 cup shredded cheddar (I utilized gentle cheddar)
- 1/4 cup chopped cured jalapenos
- 1/2 cup sharp cream

- 1 roma tomato, chopped
- Optional: serve over plain cauliflower rice (or Mexican cauliflower rice) for a more complete supper!

DIRECTIONS

1. In a pot or Dutch oven over medium heat liquefy the coconut oil. When hot, burn chicken thighs until gently brown.

2. Pour in enchilada sauce and water at that point adds onion and green chilies. Decrease heat to a stew and cover. Cook chicken for 17-25 minutes or until chicken is delicate and completely cooked through to in any event 165 degrees inner temperature.

3. Carefully eliminate the chicken and spot onto a work surface. Hack or shred chicken (your inclination) at that point add it back into the pot. Let the chicken stew uncovered for an extra 10 minutes to ingest enhance and permit the sauce to decrease a bit.

4. To Serve, top with avocado, cheddar, jalapeno, sharp cream, tomato, and some other wanted garnishes. Don't hesitate to redo these to your

inclination. Serve alone or over cauliflower rice whenever wanted simply make certain to refresh your own nourishment data depending on the situation.

Conclusion

I would like to thank you all for going through this book. All the recipes in this book are healthy meal recipes which are much beneficial. All recipes are very easy to maintain a healthy life schedule. Try these dishes at home and appreciate.

Wish you good luck!

MEAL PREP COOKBOOK
LOW CARB

Table of Contents

INTRODUCTION

Different food assortments go through different metabolic pathways in your body. They can differently affect your longing, synthetic substances and the amount of calories you burn-through. Persuading more slender is to be certain an obfuscated cycle and it requires better decision of diet plan. This book contains recipes which have low carbs and are profitable and incredible in weight decline. Following are the things which should be eaten if you need to get fit.

• Eggs are very filling and supplement thick. Diverged from refined carbs like bagels, eggs can cover desiring later in the day and may even propel weight decrease.

• Verdant greens are a glorious development to your weight decrease diet. Notwithstanding the way that they are low in calories high in fiber that helps keep you feeling full.

- Salmon is high in both protein and omega-3 unsaturated fats, making it a good choice for a strong weight decrease diet.

- Cruciferous vegetables are low in calories yet high in fiber and enhancements. Adding them to your eating routine isn't only an extraordinary weight decrease framework anyway may in like manner improve your overall prosperity.

- Eating common lean meat is a stunning technique to extend your protein confirmation. Displacing a part of the carbs or fat in your eating routine with protein could simplify it for you to lose wealth fat.

- Beans and vegetables are a decent expansion to your weight reduction diet. They're both high in protein and fiber, adding to sensations of totality and lower calorie consumption.

45. Pistachio Crusted Rack of Lamb

Prep: 10 min | Cook: 35 min | Additional: 10 min | Total: 55 min | Servings: 4 | Yield: 4 servings

INGREDIENTS

- 2 racks of lamb, trimmed
- 1 teaspoon herbes de Provence
- salt and ground black pepper to taste
- 1 tablespoon vegetable oil
- ⅔ cup chopped pistachio nuts
- 2 tablespoons dry bread crumbs
- 1 tablespoon melted butter
- 1 teaspoon olive oil
- salt and ground black pepper to taste

- 3 tablespoons Dijon mustard

DIRECTIONS

1. Step 1
2. Firstly preheat oven to 400 degrees F (200 degrees C). Line a baking sheet with aluminum foil. Generously season each stand of lamb with herbes de Provence, salt, and black pepper.
3. Step 2
4. Heat oil in a large pan over high heat. Place lamb in skillet and cook, browning on all sides, 6 to 8 minutes. Transfer lamb to a foil-lined baking sheet; set aside.
5. Step 3
6. Stir pistachios, bread crumbs, butter, olive oil, and a pinch of salt and black pepper in a bowl. Spread mustard on the fat-side of each holder of lamb. Pat pistachio mixture on top of mustard. Bake in the preheated oven until the crunch is golden and lamb is pink in the center, 20 to 25 minutes. Transfer to a plate and let rest 10 minutes before cutting.

46. Chickpeas With Dates, Turmeric, Cinnamon And Almonds

Prep time 2 Hours Serves 4

INGREDIENTS

- plum tomatoes 400g tin
- pitted dates 100g, halved
- olive oil 2 tbsp., plus extra to serve
- garlic 4 cloves, finely chopped
- Ginger finely grated to make 1 tbsp.
- coriander a small bunch, stalks and leaves separated and roughly chopped
- Ground cumin 1 tsp.
- Ground coriander 1 tsp.
- Ground turmeric 1 tsp.
- cinnamon stick 1

- lemon ½, juiced, plus 2 strips of the zest with pith removed
- large chickpeas 660g jar, rinsed and drained (or use 2 x 400g tins)
- flaked almonds 40g, toasted
- orange 1 small, cut into wedges to serve
- couscous to serve

DIRECTIONS

1. Heat the slow cooker to high or low, contingent upon wanted cooking time.
2. Put ½ the tomatoes and ½ the dates into a blender. Whizz to a purée, at that point tip into the slow cooker with the leftover tomatoes.
3. Add the oil, garlic, ginger, coriander stalks, flavors, the lemon zing and 100ml water to the slow cooker. Season and cook for 1-2 hours on high or 4-6 hours on low until the sauce is thick and rich-tasting.
4. Mix in the chickpeas and the excess dates, and cook for 30 minutes more to warm through. Add the lemon squeeze and check the flavoring by and by, adding more if important. Eliminate the lemon zing.

5. Serve the chickpeas with a shower more olive oil, the toasted almonds and chopped coriander, with the orange wedges and couscous as an afterthought.

47. Keto Pasta Milano

Preparation Time: 12-Mins | Cooking Time: 5-Mins |

Serving: 4

INGREDIENTS

- 6-ounces butter
- 18 ounces grilled chicken, cut
- 12 ounces of sun-dried tomatoes
- 12 ounces more, reduced
- 6-tablespoons of finely chopped dishes
- 36 minutes ago, there is a good example - see below
- 36 ounces bow the pasta
- 2 cups of heavy cream
- 2-tablespoons choppped garlic
- Dash salt & pepper
- 1-different types of beef or 1-beef stock cube
- 1-tablespoon of butter

DIRECTIONS

1. Make the sauce, and the guidelines are below.

2. Cook the pasta as indicated on the package.

3. Sauté butter and mushrooms for about 30 minutes. Add the raw garlic sauce and Parmesan cheese; it is amazing.

4. Drain the pasta. Add pasta to the sauté pan and mix well. Add the sliced pieces and the chosen choice, and the chosen undried cakes.

5. Garnish with a specific flavor: Serve and enjoy.

48. Slow-Cooked Brisket With Red Wine, Thyme And Onions

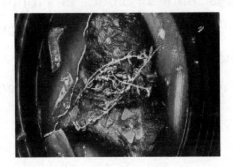

Prep time 3 Hours Serves 2

INGREDIENTS

- rolled beef brisket joint 1.5kg
- groundnut oil for frying
- onions 2, sliced
- plain flour 1 tbsp.
- red wine a large glass
- chicken stock 300ml
- Worcestershire sauce 2 tbsp.
- thyme 8 whole sprigs
- star anise 1
- carrots 2, peeled and quartered
- celery 2 sticks, quartered

DIRECTIONS

1. Heat a huge griddle until hot. Rub the joint done with oil and season truly well. Burn on all sides until brilliant, ensuring you get a pleasant dull tone. Move to the slow cooker.

2. Add the onions to similar griddle and cook for 10 minutes or until beginning to go brilliant at the edges.

3. Sprinkle over the flour, mix well and cook for 3-4 minutes. Slowly include the wine, mixing, at that point mix in the stock and Worcestershire sauce. Tip the onion blend on top of the hamburger, at that point add the thyme and star anise, and wrap up the carrots and celery.

4. Set the slow cooker to high and cook for 5 hours. Take out the brisket and put on a plate. Scoop out the carrot, celery and thyme, and dispose of. Serve the brisket with the sauce, which ought to be pleasantly thickened with the dissolved onions.

49. Beef and Guinness stew

20 Minutes + 2-3 Hours in the Oven Serves 4

INGREDIENTS

- onions 2 huge, diced
- thyme a couple of twigs
- garlic 1 clove, squashed
- olive oil
- braising meat (like hurl, cut into lumps
- plain flour 6 tbsp., very much prepared
- Guinness 500ml
- meat stock 250ml

DIRECTIONS

1. Cook the onions, thyme and garlic with a little olive oil in a huge goulash until the onion is relaxed and clear. Residue the braising steak in the prepared flour and earthy colored in a hot skillet with a little oil.

2. At the point when the hamburger has a decent, even shading, add it to the container with the onions and pour in the Guinness. Top up with the stock to simply cover the meat.

3. Cover and stew over an exceptionally low heat or move to 150C/fan 130C/gas 3 ovens for 2-3 hours until the hamburger is meltingly delicate (check following 2 hours). Season and present with squash.

4. TO MAKE IN A SLOW COOKER

5. Throw the braising steak in the prepared flour. Heat a little oil in an enormous non-stick griddle and fry the hamburger in bunches until it has a decent tone on all sides. Move to the slow cooker when sautéed. Add the Guinness to the container and let it bubble up. Scratch any caramelized bits off the lower part of the container at that point pour the entire parcel on top of the hamburger.

6. Add the remainder of the INGREDIENTS EXCEPT the hamburger stock (you will not need it as this will make the completed dish excessively fluid).

7. Give everything a mix at that point cook on low for 6 hours until the meat is delicious.

50. Sweet And Sour Chicken

Prep time 1 Hour Serves 4

INGREDIENTS

- Olive oil 1-2 tbsp.
- Skinless chicken thigh filets 500g, diced
- Red onion 1, diced
- Red pepper 1, cut
- Green pepper 1, cut
- Garlic 3 cloves, squashed
- Ginger a thumb-sized piece, finely ground
- Red chill 1, deseeded and finely chopped
- Chicken stock 400ml, just-bubbled if cooking On the hob (or 200ml if using the slow cooker)
- Delicate light brown sugar 30g
- Ketchup 4 tbsp.

- Apple juice vinegar 2 tbsp.
- Corn flour 1 tsp.
- Soy sauce 1 tbsp.

DIRECTIONS

1. Heat the oil in a hefty based dish over a medium heat. Cook the chicken for 4 minutes or until brilliant.
2. Add the onion, peppers, garlic, ginger and bean stew, and cook for 1-2 minutes. Add the stock, sugar, ketchup and vinegar; at that point give it a decent mix. Put a cover on, lessen the heat to low and cook for 45 minutes
3. Whisk together the corn flour and 1 tbsp. of water in a little bowl, at that point add to the container, blending until thickened. Not long prior to serving, add the soy sauce to taste, at that point sprinkle over the spring onions, if using.

51.   Easy Pork Stir Fry Recipe With Vegetables (Low Carb)

Cook Time: 5 minutes | Total Time: 15 minutes
Servings: 4 Calories: 226kcal

INGREDIENTS

- 3/4 pound pork loin, cut into thin strips
- 2 tablespoons avocado or olive oil (divided)
- 1 tablespoon minced fresh ginger
- 1 teaspoon minced garlic
- 12 ounces broccoli florets
- 1 red bell pepper, cut into strips
- 1 bunch green onions (scallions), cut into 2 inch pieces
- 2 tablespoons Tamari soy sauce (or coconut aminos)
- 1 tablespoon extra dry sherry

- 1 1/2 tablespoons low carb sugar (or sugar or coconut sugar)
- 1 teaspoon cornstarch (or arrowroot)
- 1 teaspoon sesame oil
- Optional INGREDIENTS
- red pepper flakes
- sesame seeds

DIRECTIONS

1. Preparation: Firstly mince a clove of garlic. Cut a 1 inch piece of ginger and peel the thin skin with a spoon. Mince the ginger and add it to the garlic. Cut the pork loin into thin shreds and mix with 1 tbsp. oil and the ginger and garlic.

2. Then cut the red bell pepper into strips and place into the bottom of a medium bowl. Cut the green onions (scallions) into 2 inch pieces, including some of the green stems and add them to the bowl. Cut the broccoli florets into large bite sized pieces, layering them on top.

3. Add the sweetener and cornstarch (arrowroot) to a small bowl and combine together. Stir in the Tamari soy sauce, dry sherry and sesame oil.

4. Method: Place the wok over high heat. It's ready when a drop of water skips across the surface. Add 1 tablespoon of oil and quickly tilt the wok to coat all surfaces. Pour out the remaining oil. Place the wok back onto the heat and begin adding the pork to the sides and bottom of the pan. Leave the pork undisturbed until it has cooked half way through; the bottom half will turn white. Stir the pork and cook until it is almost cooked through. Remove from the pan to the serving bow.

5. Dump the bowl of vegetables into the wok with the broccoli in the bottom. Cover with a lid and cook for 1 minute. Stir the vegetables and add the pork and any juices back to the pan. Stir the pork and vegetables together. Stir the stir fry sauce and pour it over the pork and vegetables. Push the pork stir fry to the sides and let the sauce boil at the bottom of the wok, stirring occasionally for numerous seconds until the sauce thickens.

6. If you would like the sauce a little thicker, remove the stir fried pork and vegetables to the serving bowl and let the sauce cook a little

longer. Pour the sauce over the stir fry when it reaches your desired level of thickness. Serve.

52. Keto Stuffed Pork Tenderloin with Mushroom Sauce

YIELD: 4 PREP TIMES: 10 MINUTES COOK TIME: 40
MINUTES TOTAL TIME: 50 MINUTES

INGREDIENTS

- 1 lb. pork tenderloin
- 2 tablespoons oil
- 3 slices provolone cheese
- 1/3 cup fresh chopped spinach
- salt and pepper to taste
- 1 teaspoon of crushed garlic
- 8 oz. of mushrooms sliced
- 1 tablespoon balsamic vinegar
- 1 large clove of garlic, minced
- 2 tablespoons butter

- 1 teaspoon Better than Bouillon, beef mixed with 1 cup water (or 1 cup beef stock)
- 1 tablespoon of heavy cream

DIRECTIONS

1. Firstly preheat oven to 375 degrees F.
2. Cut pork tenderloin lengthwise but leave 1/2 inch so you can open it like a book.
3. Plastic wrap over meat and pound thin to about 1/4 - 1/2 inch thick.
4. Drizzle minced garlic and salt and pepper over meat.
5. Layer the cheese shreds and then the spinach.
6. Tightly roll up lengthwise and secure with string or toothpicks.
7. Heat oil in a pan and brown the meat about 5 minutes on each side.
8. Place in the oven and cook about 25 minutes.
9. In the meantime add butter and mushrooms to a big sauté pan and cook for about 5 minutes.
10. Add the garlic and broth and cook for another 5 minutes until it reduces a bit.
11. Add the vinegar and combine well. Then add the cream and mix.

12. When meat comes out of the oven let sit for 10 minutes then pour mushroom sauce over top

53. Instant Pot Short Ribs

Prep: 10 mins Cook: 1 hr. 10 mins Yield: 3 servings
Calories: 860 Net Carbs: 6g

INGREDIENTS

- 2 pounds boneless beef short ribs (Note 1)
- 1 medium carrot, diced
- 1 shallot, diced
- 3 cloves garlic, minced
- 5 sprigs fresh thyme
- 1/2 cup red wine (Note 2)
- 2 tablespoons balsamic vinegar
- 1 tablespoon salted butter
- 1/2 tablespoon olive oil
- salt and pepper

DIRECTIONS

1. Prepare Short Ribs: Firstly pat short ribs dry with paper towels. Generously season all sides with salt and pepper.

2. Brown Short Ribs: Select sauté mode on pressure cooker (Note 3) for medium heat. Add olive oil to coat bottom of pot. Add butter and stir until melted. Once pot has reached temperature (display says HOT), add short ribs in single layer. Without moving them, cook for about 7 minutes until bottom is agreeably browned. Flip and cook other side for about 5 minutes. Relocate browned short ribs to plate.

3. Cook Aromatics: Add carrots, shallots, and garlic to pot. Cook for a few minutes until shallots start to brown, stirring frequently. Turn off sauté mode. Add red wine and stir, using wooden spoon to loosen flavorful brown bits stuck to bottom of pot. Add short ribs back to pot in single layer. Top with fresh thyme sprigs. Season with additional salt and pepper.

4. Pressure Cook: Secure and seal lid. Cook for 45 minutes at high pressure, followed by natural release for 15 minutes. By hand release any remaining pressure. Uncover, and

transfer only ribs to serving plates. Optionally, skim off fat in remaining liquid and discard; this will lessen amount of oil in final sauce.

5. Thicken Sauce: Turn on sauté mode and add balsamic vinegar. Boil liquid until it reduces to slightly sticky sauce, 10 to 15 minutes, stirring occasionally. Turn off sauté mode. Spoon sauce onto short ribs and serve.

54. Moroccan-Style Stuffed Peppers

40 Minutes Serves 4

INGREDIENTS

- red peppers 2 huge or 4 little, divided
- couscous 150g
- vegetable stock 300ml, just-bubbled
- chickpeas 400g tin, depleted and flushed
- feta 100g, disintegrated, in addition to extra to serve
- Sun Blush tomatoes 100g, generally chopped
- green olives 50g, chopped
- lemon ½, squeezed
- Olive oil 3 tbsp.
- coriander chopped to make 2 tbsp., in addition to extra to serve
- Rose harissa 1 tbsp.

DIRECTIONS

1. Heat the oven to 200C/fan 180C/gas 6. Put the peppers on a preparing plate, cut-side up. Cook in the oven for 20 minutes or until beginning to relax.

2. Then, put the couscous in a heatproof astound and pour the stock. Cover the bowl and leave to represent 5 minutes. Go through a fork to cushion the couscous, at that point mix through the chickpeas, feta, tomatoes, olives, lemon juice, olive oil, coriander and harissa. Season.

3. Remove the peppers from the oven and load up with the couscous blend. Get back to the oven and meal for a further 10 minutes. Present with some extra feta and coriander.

4. To cook in a slow cooker, follow stage 2 as above; at that point fill the split peppers with the couscous combination. Put them into your slow cooker and put the top on, at that point cook on the low setting for 6 hours. At that point present with the extra feta and coriander.

55. Low Carb Chili Recipe

Yield: 6 Servings | prep Time: 10 Minutes | Cook Time: 1 Hour | Total Time: 1 Hour 10 Minutes

INGREDIENTS

- 1 ½ pounds ground beef
- 1 yellow onion, diced
- 1 green pepper, diced
- 1 jalapeno, minced
- 1 clove garlic, minced
- ¼ cup tomato paste
- 15 ounces canned diced tomatoes
- 2 cups beef broth
- 2 tablespoon chili powder
- 1 teaspoon cumin
- 1 teaspoon salt

DIRECTIONS

1. Add the ground beef, onion, and bell pepper to a large deep pot and cook over medium heat, breaking up the meat as it cooks. When meat is cooked through, sewer fat from pan.

2. Add the jalapeno, garlic, tomato paste, diced tomatoes, beef broth, chili powder, cumin, and salt and stir.

3. Then bring to a boil and reduce to a simmer. Simmer for at least 20 minutes, preferably an hour for the best taste and texture.

4. Serve with sour cream and shredded cheddar, as desired

56. Low Carb Ground Beef Meal

Cook Time: 20 minutes | Total Time: 30 minutes | Servings: 6 | Calories: 360kcal

INGREDIENTS

- 500 g ground beef (1lb)
- 2 brown onions (sliced)
- 250 g button mushrooms (cut into quarters)
- 2 garlic cloves (minced)
- 1 cup beef stock
- 1 cup sour cream
- 1 tbsp. Dijon mustard
- 6 cups Shirataki noodles (optional)
- to taste salt and pepper
- for cooking oil of preference
- garnish fresh parsley (optional)

DIRECTIONS

1. Firstly in a piping hot pot, add a little bit of oil and the mushrooms and allow the mushroom to get a good sear.

2. Next, add the onion, ground beef and garlic. Season with generously with salt and pepper. Permit the ground beef to brown and the onions to soften. Stirring consistently to prevent burning. About 10 minutes.

3. Next add the Dijon mustard and the beef stock and bring to a boil.

4. Remove from heat a stir in the sour cream. Add salt if needed.

5. Enhance with fresh parsley.

57. Chili With Jalapeño Cheddar Cornbread

4 Hours 30 Minutes Serves 8

INGREDIENTS

- meat mince 750g
- onions 2 huge, finely chopped
- green chilies 2, finely chopped
- Garlic salt 1 tbsp.
- Celery salt 1 tbsp.
- Hot smoked paprika 2 tsp.
- Ground cumin 2 tsp.
- Ground cinnamon 1 tsp.
- Gentle stew powder 1 tbsp.
- Ground allspice ½ tsp.
- Dried oregano 2 tsp.
- straight leaves 2 (discretionary)
- chopped tomatoes 3 x 400g tins

- Tomato purée 2 tbsp.
- Delicate dull earthy colored sugar 2 tbsp.
- Juice vinegar 3 tbsp.
- meat stock 100ml
- ale 330ml container
- Worcestershire sauce 1 tbsp.
- dull chocolate 25g
- kidney beans 400g tin, depleted and washed
- dark beans 400g tin, depleted and washed
- CHEDDAR CORNBREAD
- solid white bread flour 70g
- moment polenta 150g
- Preparing powder 1 tbsp.
- Caster sugar 1 tbsp.
- eggs 3
- entire milk 375ml
- unsalted spread 75g, softened, in addition to extra for the tin
- develop cheddar 100g, ground
- cured jalapeños cuts from a container 6, chopped

DIRECTIONS:

1. Heat a huge griddle at that point fry the mince in clumps ensuring each group is very much sautéed for certain fresh pieces. Tip each bunch into a slow cooker when wrapped up.

2. Add the wide range of various INGREDIENTS aside from the beans and cook on high for 4 hours (or low for 8 hours). Add the beans and cook for an additional 30 minutes.

3. Then, to make the cornbread, heat the oven to 220C/fan 200C/gas 7. Margarine and line a 900g portion tin with heating paper. Blend the dry INGREDIENTS in a bowl with 11/2 tsp. of salt. Whisk the eggs, milk and dissolved spread together. Add the wet INGREDIENTS to the dry and blend. Mix in the cheddar and jalapeños. It will be very slender however doesn't stress, the polenta absorb everything in the oven.

4. Fill the portion tin and cook for 15 minutes, at that point turn the oven down to 200C/fan 180C/gas 6 and cook for an additional 25 minutes or until a stick tells the truth (cover with foil in the event that it goes dull excessively fast). Cool totally in the tin at that point end up. Serve cuts with the stew – in the

event that you need to serve it warm, cut, heat through in a hot oven, covered with foil, for 10 minutes.

58. Low Carb Lamb & Beef Meal

Active: 25 mins Total: 40 mins Servings: 4

INGREDIENTS

- Ingredient Checklist
- 1 ½ cups water
- 1 cup brown basmati rice
- 8 ounces lean ground beef
- 8 ounces ground lamb
- 3 cups chopped yellow onions
- 2 tablespoons chopped garlic
- 1 tablespoon ground turmeric (see Tip)
- 2 teaspoons grated fresh ginger
- 1 ½ teaspoons ground coriander
- 1 teaspoon ground cumin
- 3 tablespoons tomato paste
- 3 cups unsalted beef broth
- 2 tablespoons Worcestershire sauce

- ¾ teaspoon salt
- ¼ cup low-fat plain Greek yogurt
- 3 tablespoons chopped fresh cilantro

DIRECTIONS

1. Step 1
2. Mix water and rice in a medium saucepan; bring to a boil over high heat. Reduce heat to a simmer, cover and cook until the water is absorbed, about 40 minutes.
3. Step 2
4. Meanwhile, cook beef and lamb in a large skillet over medium-high heat, crumbling with a wooden spoon, until no longer pink, 5 to 6 minutes. Add onions and cook, stirring occasionally, until translucent, 6 to 8 minutes.
5. Step 3
6. Increase heat to high. Add garlic, turmeric, ginger, coriander and cumin; cook, stirring, until fragrant, about 1 minute. Stir in tomato paste and cook, stirring, for 1 minute. Stir in broth, Worcestershire and salt; bring to a boil. Reduce heat to medium and simmer, stirring sporadically, until thickened, 13 to 15 minutes.

7. Step 4

8. Present the meal over the rice, topped with some yogurt and cilantro with naan bread on the side.

59. Low Carb Paleo Beef Liver Recipe

Prep Time: 10 minutes Cook Time: 30 minutes Total Time: 40 minutes Servings: 4 servings Calories: 297kcal

INGREDIENTS

- 1 pound grass-fed beef liver
- 4 strips bacon we use Garrett Valley Uncured Bacon
- 3 tbsp. pasture butter divided use
- ½ large Onion
- 4 large garlic cloves
- 10 ounces sliced button mushrooms

DIRECTIONS

1. Unpack the beef liver and lay flat on a layer of paper towels. Pat dry.

2. Salt and pepper the liver generously, and leave it out at room temperature while you make the remaining INGREDIENTS.

3. Dice bacon and fry in 2 tablespoons of butter in a large skillet. When crispy, remove the bacon bits from the pan and drain on paper towels. Leave the grease and butter in the pan.

4. Slice onion roughly. You want your pieces of onion to be similar in size to a bite of liver. The one-to-one ratio is part of the flavor secret! Sauté on low in bacon oil and butter until it starts to soften but is not yet translucent.

5. Easy Beef Liver Recipe

6. Firstly add garlic to the onions for an additional 30 seconds.

7. Add mushrooms to the onions and garlic. Sauté everything until mushrooms is tender.

8. Simple Liver Recipe

9. Shove all the vegetables to one side of the pan, away from heat. You may want to scoot the pan so that side is off the burner a bit.

10. Turn the heat up to medium and add the last tablespoon of butter.

11. When the butter is melted, add half the liver slices. Cook until you start to see the edges cooking. They'll turn from red to gray. When that border is a few millimeters thick (2-3 minutes, or so), flip them over.

12. Fry on the second side for another 2-3 minutes. Until you know how you like your liver, the best way to check is to cut into it. If it's still red, keep until it is just barely cooked through. You want just a tinge of pink so it's cooked but still tender.

13. Place liver on a platter and cook remaining liver in the same fashion.

14. Toss the bacon bits with the vegetables and smother the liver with them.

60. Low Carb Shepherds Pie

Servings 8 servings' calories per serving 350kcal

prep time: 30 minutes cook time: 30 minutes

INGREDIENTS:

- FILLING
- 1 tbsp. coconut oil
- 1.5 lbs. ground beef/lamb
- 1/2 cup onion, diced
- 2 stalks celery, diced
- 1 large carrot, diced
- 2 cloves garlic, minced
- 1 tsp. rosemary
- 1 tsp. thyme
- 1.5 tsp. pink Himalayan salt
- 1/2 tsp. black pepper
- 1 cup chicken broth

- 2 tbsp. tomato paste
- 1-2 tbsp. Worcestershire sauce
- MASHED CAULIFLOWER TOPPING
- 1 large cauliflower head, cut into small florets, steamed (see video above on how to steam cauliflower)
- 1 cup shredded cheddar cheese
- 2 tbsp. cream cheese, softened
- 2 tbsp. heavy cream
- 2 tbsp. butter, softened
- 2 cloves garlic
- 1/2 tsp. pink Himalayan salt
- 1/4 tsp. black pepper
- fresh parsley, garnish

DIRECTIONS:

1. Firstly heat oil in a large pan over medium-high heat. Add beef (or lamb) and cook until no longer pink, breaking it up with a wooden spoon and stirring recurrently, about 5 minutes.

2. Add cubed onions, celery, carrots, garlic, and seasonings to the pan. Cook until the

vegetables soften, about 5 minutes, stirring occasionally.

3. Add broth, tomato paste, and Worcestershire sauce to the pan, stirring until the paste dissolves. Reduce heat slightly and let it continue to simmer until the sauce thickens, about 15 minutes, before turning off the heat.

4. Preheat oven to 400 degrees F.

5. Place steamed cauliflower to a food processor or blender. Add ½ cup cheddar cheese, cream cheese, cream, butter, garlic, salt, and pepper. Puree until smooth consistency, scraping the sides as necessary (See video above for steps on how to steam the cauliflower).

6. Allocate meat and veggie mixture to a 2-quart baking dish, spreading it in an even layer.

7. Spread the mashed cauliflower evenly over the meat, then top with remaining shredded cheddar cheese.

8. Bake for 30 minutes, or until the peaks of the mashed cauliflower are browned. Remove from oven and cool slightly, then garnish with parsley, if desired. Serve immediately.

61. Ginger Beef Noodle Soup

Prep time: 15 min Serves: 2

INGREDIENTS

- Marinated hamburger
- 1 tablespoon sesame oil
- 2 teaspoons soy sauce
- 2 cloves garlic, minced
- 2 teaspoons ginger, stripped and minced
- ½ teaspoon salt
- ½ teaspoon white pepper
- 1 pound top sirloin, meagerly cut
- flavor-injected stock
- 2 quarts in addition to 1 cup top caliber (no salt added) hamburger stock
- 2 cinnamon sticks
- 1 star anise

- 6 cloves garlic, crushed
- 1 (1 inch) piece ginger, stripped and meagerly cut
- salt and pepper to taste
- gathering
- 12 ounces dry chuka soba noodles
- 2 tablespoons additional virgin olive oil
- 1 pack infant spinach
- 1 pack infant kale
- cilantro twigs
- chili drops

DIRECTIONS:

1. Join all marinade INGREDIENTS into a little combining bowl and race as one. Spot hamburger into a shallow heating dish and pour marinade over meat. Flip meat to cover the opposite side. Cover with saran wrap and put in a safe spot for at any rate 30 minutes and as long as 60 minutes.

2. For stock: Pour stock into an enormous pot and add aromatics. Stew for around 60 minutes. Strain, season with salt and pepper and put in a safe spot.

3. Fill an enormous pot with water and spot over high heat. Heat water to the point of boiling. Add chuka soba noodles to the bubbling water and bubble for 1 moment. Eliminate from heat and cover for 5 minutes. Channel and put noodles in a safe spot.

4. Spot a sauté skillet over medium-high heat and add oil. Blotch the meat dry with a paper towel and burn the pieces on each side for 2 to 3 minutes. Eliminate from heat and put in a safe spot.

5. Heat flavor injected stock to the point of boiling and add spinach and kale a season with salt and pepper. Bubble for 2 minutes, and then add noodles. Add half of the hamburger and keep on bubbling for 2 to 3 minutes. Season with salt and pepper.

6. To serve: Dish out equivalent servings of the soup, top each with a couple of cuts of the leftover meat and top with cilantro and bean stew drops, whenever wanted. Serve.

62. Low Carb Steak Bites

*Prep Time: 10 mins Cook Time: 10 mins Total Time:
20 mins, 5 servings*

INGREDIENTS

- 1 3/4 pounds flank steak
- 1/4 cup soy sauce
- 2 tablespoons nectar
- 1 tablespoon stew paste
- 1-2 tablespoons light seasoned olive oil

DIRECTIONS

1. Cut the steak across the grain into strips 1/2"
   wide. Cut each strip into reduced down pieces,
   roughly 1/2" – 3/4" in size. Spot the pieces of
   hamburger into a medium size bowl. Mix
   together the soy sauce, nectar, and bean stew
   paste. Pour over the meat and mix to cover

well. Allow the meat to marinate for 20-30 minutes.

2. Heat a substantial base hardened steel dish or wok over medium high heat. At the point when the dish is hot, add 1 tablespoon of oil and twirl to cover. Add 1/3 of the meat to the container and spread out in a solitary layer. Allow it to cook for about a moment, until the meat has carmelized. Flip the meat or throw with a spatula for an extra moment or two as it completes the process of cooking. Eliminate the meat from the dish to a plate.

3. Add half of the excess meat to the hot dish and rehash the above advances. Add the cooked meat to the holding up plate. In the event that vital, add the excess tablespoon of oil to the skillet prior to adding the leftover meat. Rehash the means. Enjoy!

4. In the event that anytime the skillet starts to smoke, it is excessively hot. Lower the heat marginally and keep cooking. Eliminate the steak chomps from the container when they are seared outwardly and still delicious within. They will keep cooking briefly after they are

taken out from the heat. Skirt steak might be filling in for the flank steak in this formula.

63. Low Carb Beef Salad With Asian Slaw

Prep Time: 20 mins Cook Time: 20 mins Total Time: 40 mins Servings: 4 servings | Calories: 384kcal

INGREDIENTS

- Marinated Beef
- 320 g sirloin steak (approx. 2 steaks – fat eliminated)
- 2 tbsp. clam sauce
- 1 tsp. dim soy sauce
- 1 tbsp. corn flour
- 1 tbsp. sunflower oil
- Crunchy Slaw
- 400 g white cabbage (meagerly destroyed)
- 160 g mange promote (finely cut)
- 1 medium carrot (cut into fine cudgel)

- 1 red onion (finely cut)
- 1 red pepper (finely cut)
- Slaw Dressing
- 2 tbsp. sunflower oil
- 1 tbsp. light soy sauce
- 4 tbsp. rice wine vinegar (can substitute with red wine vinegar)
- 2 tbsp. lime juice
- 2 tsp. sesame oil
- 1 clove garlic squashed
- 1 red bean stew (de-cultivated and finely cut)
- 1 tbsp. root ginger (finely ground)
- 1 tbsp. mint leaves (finely destroyed)
- To Serve
- 2 little jewel lettuce (forgets about isolated)
- 4 spring onions (finely cut)
- 4 tbsp. peanuts (squashed)
- 1 lime (cut into wedges)
- 1 little bundle new mint leaves

DIRECTIONS:

1. Marinated Beef
2. Spot the clam sauce, dim soy sauce and corn flour into a bowl and blend well to join to a smooth paste. Add the entire sirloin steaks to

the marinade and blend to guarantee the steaks are totally covered. Put in a safe spot for 15 minutes while you set up the remainder of the dish.

3. Asian Slaw

4. Set up every one of the vegetables for the Asian slaw and spot them in an enormous bowl. Put in a safe spot.

5. In a bowl combine as one every one of the INGREDIENTS for the slaw dressing and mix well to join. Pour over the vegetables and blend completely through the vegetables. Put to the side until prepared to serve.

6. To serve

7. At the point when prepared to serve, place a huge non-stick griddle over a high heat. Add 1tbsp sunflower oil to the griddle and spot the steaks into the skillet to cook for 2-3 minutes on each side. The timeframe will change contingent upon the thickness of the steaks. However, for a medium cooked steak you are searching for an interior temperature of 60-65C.

8. At the point when the steak is cooked, eliminate from the container and put to the side on a warm plate to rest for 5 minutes.

9. In the interim set up the lettuce leaves and spot a spoon of the slaw into every one of the leaves.

10. When rested cut every sirloin steak into slender cuts and a few cuts onto every lettuce leaf. Trimming with spring onion, squashed peanuts, new torn mint leaves and a wedge of new lime. Serve right away.

11. On the off chance that you don't care for bean stew avoid it with regards to the dressing completely.

12. The trimming things are a serving idea in particular. In the event that you have a nut hypersensitivity leaves the nuts off the dish.

64. Low Carb Fish Fillets With Vegetable Sticks

Prep time: 20 min Serving 3

INGREDIENTS

- 4 halibut or other firm-fleshed white fish fillets (total 11/2 lb./750 g)
- 2 tbsp. low-sodium soy sauce
- 2 tbsp. white wine or sake
- small knob peeled fresh ginger minced
- medium carrots cut into long matchsticks
- oz. snow peas cut in halves lengthwise
- 1/2 yellow bell pepper

DIRECTIONS

1. Firstly Place fillets in a small, shallow baking dish that will fit inside a large, deep skillet. In a small bowl, stir together soy sauce and wine. Put over fish. Top with ginger and carrots; set aside.

2. Now fill skillet with about an inch of water. Bring to a simmer. Place a wire rack in the skillet.

3. Place baking dish containing the fish on the wire rack, and cover. Steam these for five to six minutes.

4. Add snow peas and yellow pepper to the baking dish and again cover it. Steam until fish flakes when touched with a fork and vegetables are crisp-tender, about five minutes. Present immediately.

65. Low Carb Asian Chicken

Prep: 5 Min | Cook: 8 Min, Serving: 8

INGREDIENTS

- CHICKEN:
- 500g/1lb breast filets, skinless and boneless (2 huge) (Note 1 different cuts)
- 1/2 tsp. each salt and pepper
- 1/2 tbsp. rice flour, or universally handy/plain flour (Note 2)
- 1 1/2 tbsp. oil , vegetable or canola
- SAUCE:
- tsp. sesame oil
- garlic cloves , finely minced
- 2 tsp. ginger , finely minced
- 1 tsp. bean stew chips/red pepper pieces (decrease for less fiery)

- 1/2 cup water
- tbsp. sriracha (sub ketchup for not fiery, Note 3)
- 1 tbsp. soy sauce , light or universally handy (Note 4)
- 1/4 cup nectar (sub brown sugar)
- 3 tbsp. lime juice (sub 2 tbsp. rice vinegar)
- Enhancements (CHOOSE):
- Green onion (finely cut), sesame seeds, new stew, lime wedges

DIRECTIONS:

1. CHICKEN:
2. Season: Cut every chicken bosom fifty-fifty on a level plane to frame 4 steaks absolute. Sprinkle each side with salt, pepper and rice flour, shaking off overabundance.
3. Sear: Heat oil in a huge skillet over high heat. Add chicken and cook for 2 minutes. Turn and cook the opposite side for 2 minutes, at that point eliminate to a plate.
4. Tacky Chili SAUCE:

5. Sesame oil: Allow the skillet to cool somewhat then re-visitation of the oven on medium. Add sesame oil and heat.

6. Garlic and ginger: Add garlic and ginger, cook for 15 seconds.

7. Bean stews chips: Add stew pieces and cook for 30 seconds until garlic is brilliant.

8. Sriracha, soy and nectar: Turn heat up to medium-high. Add water, sriracha, soy sauce and nectar, mix well, scratching the base of the dish to break down every one of the brilliant pieces into the fluid.

9. Stew for 2 minutes until it decrease to a thick syrup. Add lime juice, at that point stew for a further 30 seconds until it thickens back to thick syrup.

10. Coat chicken: Turn heat off. Return chicken to dish, going to cover in sauce.

11. Serve chicken, finishing off with residual sauce in skillet, embellished with green onions, sesame seed and additional lime wedges, whenever wanted.

12. Formula Notes:

13. Chicken – Boneless and skinless thighs and tenderloins additionally work, utilize 500g/1lb.

Try not to slice down the middle, utilize entire pieces.

14. Thighs will take more time to cook through, around 4 minutes on the primary side, 3 minutes on the subsequent side;

15. Tenderloins are (commonly) more modest so they should take the around a similar time as bosom.

16. Inside temperature of cooked chicken:

17. Bosom and tenderloin: 65°C/150°F

18. Thigh: 75°C/167°F

19. Rice flour – Yields a decent, firm outside layer onto which the tacky stew sauce sticks. Without it, the sauce simply sneaks off the chicken. It is anything but a serious deal in the event that you don't have it – sub plain/generally useful flour. Rice flour is simply somewhat crisper. ☺

20. Sriracha – This adds fieriness just as different flavors like vinegar and garlic into the sauce, in addition to it thickens the sauce.

21. On the off chance that you need less zesty, sub some of it with ketchup. In the event that you sub every last bit of it, the dish turns out

to be very sweet so add a scramble of additional lime to redress (it's likewise absolutely not what this formula is proposed to be, but rather it's as yet delicious!)

22. In the event that you need fiery however don't have sriracha, additionally sub with ketchup in addition to some other hot sauce to taste, or cayenne pepper or more stew chips.

23. Soy sauce – Use universally handy or light, don't utilize dim soy sauce (shading and flavor excessively extraordinary). More on various soy sauces here.

24. Capacity – Lean meats like bosom and tenderloin are in every case best served newly made. However, it will save for 3 – 4 days in the cooler. Best to reheat in the microwave, and delicately, so you don't overcook it!

66. Low Carb Asparagus With Hollandaise Sauce

Prep Time: 10 minutes | Cook Time: 5 minutes | Total Time: 15 minutes | Servings: 4 Calories: 248kcal

INGREDIENTS

- pound asparagus, trimmed
- 1 tablespoon water
- salt and pepper to taste
- Hollandaise Sauce
- 4 ounces salted butter
- large egg yolks
- 1/2 teaspoon Dijon mustard
- 1 tablespoon water
- 1-2 teaspoons freshly squeezed lemon juice (or white vinegar)
- 1-2 pinch cayenne pepper
- 1-2 pinch white pepper

DIRECTIONS

1. Preparation:
2. If the asparagus is medium to large in wideness, cut 1 inch off of the bottoms and lightly peel the stalks with a vegetable peeler. I start about 1/3 from the top and continue to the bottom of each spear. If the asparagus is thin, hold a spike towards the bottom and bend it until it snaps. Cut the remaining spears to the same length. Discrete the eggs, reserving the whites for another use.
3. Asparagus:
4. Put the asparagus in a microwave safe bowl and add 1 tablespoon of water. Cover with plastic wrap and cook at high power from 1 1/2 - 2 1/2 minutes depending on your microwave. Drain off the water and keep covered. Alternately, blanch the asparagus in boiling water until it is crunchy tender, drain, and keep warm.
5. Blender Hollandaise
6. Add the egg yolks, 1 tablespoon of water, 1 teaspoon of lemon juice and the mustard to a blender. Place the lid on top and remove the middle piece. Place the butter in a medium to

large frying pan and melt the butter over medium heat. Turn the heat up to medium high and slightly swirl the pan every few moments. When the solids in the bottom of the pan just begin to turn brown, turn off the heat. Turn the blender on low and begin pouring the hot butter into the blender, leaving the brown solids behind in the pan.

7. After the butter has been incorporated, add the cayenne pepper and white pepper and blend. Taste. Adjust seasoning with more acid, salt or pepper. Pour over the asparagus and serve immediately.

67. Kemal Curry (Low Carb)

Yield: Serves 4 Prep Time: 10 Minutes Cook Time: 40 Minutes Total Time: 50 Minutes

INGREDIENTS

- 450g (1lb) of extra lean beef mince
- large onion, chopped finely
- 1 large carrot, finely chopped
- 1 stalk of celery, finely chopped
- cloves of garlic, crushed
- 1 heaped teaspoon of fresh grated ginger
- teaspoons of cumin seeds
- 2 teaspoon of ground coriander
- 1 teaspoon of deggi mirch Chilli Powder (can add more if you like it really spicy).
- 1 teaspoon of garam masala

- 1 teaspoon of turmeric
- 1 cup of frozen peas
- tablespoons of tomato paste
- 2.5 cups (600ml) of beef stock (use just 1.5 cups for instant pot)
- freshly chopped coriander to serve
- salt and black pepper
- cooking oil spray (I used avocado)

DIRECTIONS

1. Stove Top:
2. Spray a frying pan over a medium heat with some spray oil
3. Add the onion, garlic, carrot, celery and ginger and cook for approx. 5 mins to soften.
4. Add the minced beef and cook until browned, breaking up large pieces with the back of a wooden ladle while it cooks.
5. Stir in all the spices (plus the green chilli's if using) and tomato paste and mix to evenly coat.
6. Add the stock and bring to a boil, then reduce heat to a simmer until meat is cooked through

and stock has reduced to a thicker consistency – approx. 30mins

7. Stir in the peas at the last few minutes.
8. Taste and season as needed with salt and black pepper.
9. Serve topped with freshly chopped coriander and steamed rice.
10. Instant Pot:
11. Set instant pot to sauté mode
12. Add ground beef, onion, celery, carrot, garlic and ginger
13. Fry till beef is browned.
14. Add all other INGREDIENTS (expect peas and coriander)
15. Switch to 12 minutes (high) and ensure valve is closed.
16. When it honks to signal it has done cooking, open the valve to quickly release the pressure.
17. Switch to sauté mode again and simmer for about 1-2 mins just to heat through the peas.
18. Taste and season as needed with salt and black pepper.
19. Serve with chopped fresh coriander and your choice of sides.

68. Low-Carb Beef Bourguignon Stew

Prep Time 30 minutes Cook Time 30 minutes

Total Time 1 hour Servings 6

INGREDIENTS

- 4 slices bacon Sliced crosswise
- 1/2 pound stew meat cut into 1 1/2 -2 inch cubes and dried with a paper towel
- 4 ounces white onion (about 1 small)
- stalks celery sliced
- 8 ounces mushrooms thickly sliced
- 1 clove garlic crushed
- 1/2 teaspoon xanthan gum
- 1 cup dry burgundy wine
- 1 cup beef stock (or low-salt broth)
- tablespoons tomato paste
- 1/2 teaspoon dried thyme
- 1 bay leaf

- 1/2 teaspoon sea salt (or to taste)
- 1/4 teaspoon black pepper freshly ground
- 1 tablespoon fresh parsley chopped

DIRECTIONS

1. Instant Pot DIRECTIONS:
2. With cover off of the Instant Pot, choose the sauté setting. When the "hot" indications shows, add the bacon. Cook bacon, stirring occasionally, until crisp. Remove to a paper towel lined plate. Do not discard bacon grease.
3. Add half of the beef to the Instant Pot. Pieces should not be touching. Drizzle with salt and pepper. Allow the first side brown before turning. Brown all sides and remove to a plate. Repeat for the other half of the meat. If the Instant Pot turns off during this process, set it to Sauté once again.
4. Abandon all but 1 tablespoon of drippings from the pot. (If there is less than 1 tablespoon, add about a tablespoon of butter or preferred oil to the Instant Pot) Continuing on the sauté setting, add onion and celery to the pot. Allow to cook until just starting to soften. Add

mushrooms. Cook vegetables until mushrooms start to soften. Stir in garlic and cook for one minute. Transfer it to a plate

5. If there isn't any oil left in the pot, add about a teaspoon. Add xanthan gum to the pot. Stir to distribute oil through the xanthan gum. Pour in burgundy and stir, scraping up browned bits. Bring to a simmer and simmer until wine starts to condense. Add beef broth. Stir in tomato paste, thyme and bay leaf. Bring to a simmer. Allow to simmer until broth has thickened enough to coat a spoon. Return vegetables browned chunks of beef (along with the drippings), and bacon to the pot. Stir in salt and pepper.

6. Cover Instant Pot. Position steam release handles to "Sealing". Choose the Meat/Stew function and press +/- buttons to adjust time to 30 minutes. When stew is done, use the Quick Release method (consult Instant Pot instruction manual) to vent the Instant Pot. Press Cancel. Be sure the float valve is down before opening the lid.

7. Taste and adjust seasoning. Remove bay leaf and sprinkle with parsley before serving.

8. Slow cooker DIRECTIONS: (add 5 hours and 30 minutes to cooking time)

9. Heat a large soup pot or Dutch oven over medium high heat. When the pot is hot, add the bacon. Cook bacon, stirring occasionally, until crisp. Remove to a paper towel lined plate to drain then transfer to the slow-cooker

10. Add half of the beef to the pot. Chunks should not be touching. Sprinkle with salt and pepper. Allow the first side brown before turning. Brown all sides then transfer to the slow-cooker. Repeat for the other half of the meat.

11. Discard all but 1 tablespoon of drippings from the pot. If there is less than a tablespoon, add a bit of your choice of oil. Continuing over medium-high heat, add onion and celery to the pot. Allow to cook until just starting to soften. Add mushrooms. Cook vegetables until mushrooms start to soften. Stir in garlic and cook for one minute. Allocate vegetables to the crock pot.

12. If there is no oil left in the pot, add about a teaspoon of oil of your choice. Add xanthan gum to the pot. Stir to divide all in the oil. Pour in burgundy and stir, scraping up browned bits.

Bring to a simmer and simmer until wine starts to thicken. Add beef broth. Stir in tomato paste, thyme and bay leaf. Bring to a simmer. Permit to simmer until broth has thickened enough to coat a spoon. Stir in salt and pepper. Transfer to the slow-cooker and stir together with the bacon, beef and the vegetables.

13. Cover the slow-cooker. Cook stew on low 6-8 hours or until meat is fall-apart tender.

14. Before serving, taste and adjust seasoning. Remove bay leaf and drizzle with parsley before serving.

69. Low Carb Sage-Rubbed Salmon

Total Time Prep/Total Time: 20 min. Makes 6 servings

INGREDIENTS

- 2 tablespoons minced new savvy
- teaspoon garlic powder
- 1 teaspoon fit salt
- 1 teaspoon newly ground pepper
- 1 skin-on salmon filet (1-1/2 pounds)
- tablespoons olive oil

DIRECTIONS

1. Preheat oven to 375°. Blend initial 4 INGREDIENTS; rub onto substance side of salmon. Cut into 6 segments.

2. In a large cast-iron skillet, heat oil over medium heat. Add salmon, skin side down; cook 5 minutes. Move skillet to oven; heat just until fish drops effectively with a fork, around 10 minutes.

70. Low Carb Parmesan Roasted Broccoli

Total Time Prep/Total Time: 30 min. Makes 4 servings

INGREDIENTS

- 2 little broccoli crowns (around 8 ounces each)
- 3 tablespoons olive oil
- 1/2 teaspoon salt
- 1/2 teaspoon pepper
- 1/4 teaspoon squashed red pepper chips
- 4 garlic cloves, daintily cut
- 2 tablespoons ground Parmesan cheddar
- teaspoon ground lemon zing

DIRECTIONS

1. Preheat oven to 425°. Cut broccoli crowns into quarters through and through. Shower with oil; sprinkle with salt, pepper and pepper drops. Spot in a material lined 15x10x1-in. skillet.

2. Broil until fresh delicate, 10-12 minutes. Sprinkle with garlic; cook 5 minutes longer. Sprinkle with cheddar; broil until cheddar is dissolved and stalks of broccoli are delicate, 2-4 minutes more. Sprinkle with lemon zing.

71. Low Carb Spicy Pork Brussels Bowls

Prep Time: 5 Mins Cook Time: 25 Mins Total Time: 30 Mins Yield: 4 Servings Course: Dinner, Lunch, Meal Prep

INGREDIENTS

- olive oil spray
- pound 90% lean ground pork, or swap it for a meatless ground meat option
- tablespoons red wine vinegar
- cloves garlic, minced
- 1 teaspoon smoky paprika
- 2 teaspoons ancho chili powder
- 1 teaspoon kosher salt
- 1/4 teaspoon cayenne pepper
- 1/4 teaspoon freshly ground black pepper
- 1/4 teaspoon dried oregano

- 1/4 teaspoon ground cumin
- 6 cups shredded Brussels sprouts
- 1/4 cup chopped onion
- large eggs

DIRECTIONS

1. Heat a large cast iron or heavy nonstick skillet over medium heat, spray with oil and cook the meat, breaking it up in small pieces.
2. Combine spices in a small bowl.
3. spices
4. Add garlic, season with spices and vinegar and cook until browned and no longer pink in the middle, 8 to 10 minutes.
5. ground pork in a skillet
6. Set it aside on a plate.
7. Add the Brussels and onions to the pan and cook over high heat, stirring occasionally until the Brussels start to brown and are tender crisp, 6 to 7 minutes.
8. Return the pork to the skillet and mix everything together 1 to 2 minutes.
9. Heat a nonstick skillet or pan and spray with oil, when hot cook the eggs, covered until the

whites are just set and the yolks are still runny, 2 to 3 minutes.

72. Cheesy Keto Casserole

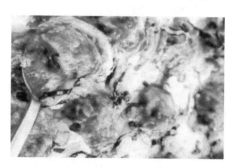

Prep Time: 5 mins Cook Time: 40 mins Total Time: 45 mins

INGREDIENTS

- For the meatballs:
- 2 lb. ground beef
- 1/2 cup grated parmesan cheese
- 3/4 cup shredded mozzarella cheese
- egg
- 1/4 cup grated onion
- garlic cloves, minced
- Tbsp. chopped fresh parsley
- 1/2 tsp. onion powder
- 1/2 tsp. garlic powder
- 1/2 tsp. Italian seasoning
- Salt and pepper, to taste
- For the casserole:

- 1 (24 oz.) jar favorite marinara sauce (I prefer Rao's)
- 1/2 cup ricotta cheese
- 1/2 cup shredded mozzarella cheese
- 2 to 3 Tbsp. fresh basil, chopped

DIRECTIONS

1. Firstly preheat oven to 400 degrees F.
2. To make the meatballs: In a large bowl combine ground beef, cheeses, egg, onion, garlic, parsley and seasonings, combining well. Use a cookie scoop to form the meatballs so they are all the same size, rolling them around in your hands, and arrange on a baking dish or cookie sheet. You should get about 15 to 16 large meatballs.
3. Bake meatballs for 20 to 25 minutes, or until fully cooked. Remove meatballs, draining any excess grease, and assemble cooked meatballs in a baking dish.
4. Pour marinara sauce evenly over the meatballs and spoon ricotta cheese on top. Sprinkle with mozzarella cheese and bake in the oven for

about 15 minutes until cheese is melted and bubbly.

5. Remove from oven and top with fresh basil. Serve and enjoy!

73. Low Carb Lamb Curry Recipe

Cook Time: 1 hr. 20 mins Total Time: 2 hrs. 35 mins

Servings: 14 serve Calories: 480kcal

INGREDIENTS

- Marinade
- 2 teaspoons Ginger finely chopped or crushed
- 3 cloves garlic crushed
- 2 teaspoons Cumin ground
- 2 teaspoons coriander ground
- teaspoon onion powder
- 1 teaspoon cardamom ground
- 1 teaspoon Paprika ground
- 1 teaspoon turmeric ground
- 1 teaspoon Kashmiri Chili Powder
- tablespoons olive oil
- Curry
- pounds lamb shoulder diced

- tablespoons Ghee
- 1 medium Onion diced
- 1 teaspoon cinnamon ground
- 1 teaspoon Kashmiri Chili Powder
- 2 teaspoons Salt
- 1 teaspoon Pepper
- 1 cup Heavy Cream
- 1/2 cup flaked almonds
- 3 tablespoons Cilantro roughly chopped

DIRECTIONS

1. Marinade
2. In a mixing bowl combine all marinade INGREDIENTS.
3. Add the diced lamb and mix well.
4. Store in the fridge to marinate for at least 1 hour, or overnight.
5. Curry
6. In a large saucepan add the ghee and place over medium heat.
7. Add the onion, cinnamon & chili powder and sauté for 3 minutes.
8. Add the marinated lamb, salt and pepper and stir to ensure that lamb is browning.

9. Allow the lamb to cook for 10 minutes before adding the cream and reducing the heat to low.

10. Simmer the curry, partially covered, for 1 hour. Check the lamb for tenderness. If the lamb is tough continue cooking until tender.

11. Remove the lid and simmer for another 10 minutes.

12. Add the flaked almonds and stir well. Add any extra seasoning.

13. Remove from the heat, garnish with coriander and serve.

74. Low Carb Cabbage Cake Recipe

Serves: 6 servings Prep time: 45 minutes Cook time: 45 minutes Total time: 1 hr. 30 mins

INGREDIENTS

- head of savoy cabbage (or green cabbage)
- pounds ground beef
- onion (finely diced)
- red bell pepper (diced)
- green bell pepper (diced)
- cloves garlic (minced)
- 1 teaspoon dried basil
- 1 tablespoon Worcestershire sauce
- 1 cup grated Romano (or parmesan cheese)
- 1 cup ricotta cheese
- 1/2 cup marinara sauce (plus extra for topping)

- cups shredded mozzarella cheese
- egg
- tablespoons olive oil
- 1 tablespoon fresh basil (chopped)
- 1 tablespoon fresh parsley (chopped)
- salt and pepper

DIRECTIONS

1. Firstly preheat oven to 350 degrees F.
2. Core and discrete the leaves from the cabbage, then cook them in boiling water for 5 minutes. Drain well, pat dry, and set aside.
3. Grease the bottom and sides of a 9-inch spring form pan with olive oil, and arrange the largest leaves on the lowest so they cover the bottom and sides of the pan all around.
4. Place a large skillet over medium-high heat and the meat and cook breaking it with a wooden spoon, until no longer pink, sewer the grease and set aside the beef.
5. Add the olive oil, once hot add the onion, peppers, garlic, and dried basil, cook, and toss until the veggies are tender about 5 minutes.

Add the cooked meat and stir to combine. Season with salt and pepper.

6. Add Worcestershire sauce, grated parmesan cheese, ricotta, and marinara, fresh basil, and parsley, cook for another 5-7 minutes, set aside, and let it cool then mix in the egg.

7. Add the first layer of meat mixture down; add shredded mozzarella cheese, next layer a cabbage leaf on top to cover the meat mixture. Repeat until you reach the top or run out of filling.

8. Finish with cabbage leaves on top and tuck them in the dish all around.

9. Drizzle the top with a bit of olive oil, salt, and pepper, and some parmesan cheese.

10. Bake in the preheated oven for about 40-50 minutes.

11. Let it rest for 15-20 minutes, then remove the sides of the spring form pan.

12. Cut into slices and serve with more warmed marinara sauce, parsley, and grated cheese.

75. Low Carb Smoky Cauliflower Bites

Total Time Prep/Total Time: 20 min. Makes 4 servings

INGREDIENTS

- 3 tablespoons olive oil
- 3/4 teaspoon sea salt
- teaspoon paprika
- 1/2 teaspoon ground cumin
- 1/4 teaspoon ground turmeric
- 1/8 teaspoon chili powder
- medium head cauliflower, broken into florets

DIRECTIONS

1. Firstly preheat oven to 450°. Mix first 6 INGREDIENTS. Add cauliflower florets; toss to coat. Transfer to a 15x10x1-in. baking pan. Roast until tender, 15-20 minutes, stirring halfway.

76. Low Carb Avocado Crab Boats

Total Time Prep/Total Time: 20 min. Makes 8 servings

INGREDIENTS

- 5 medium ready avocados, stripped and divided
- 1/2 cup mayonnaise
- 2 tablespoons lemon juice
- 2 jars (6 ounces each) bump crabmeat, depleted
- 4 tablespoons chopped new cilantro, separated
- 2 tablespoons minced chives
- 1/4 teaspoon pepper
- 1/2 teaspoon paprika
- Lemon wedges

DIRECTIONS

1. Preheat oven. Spot 2 avocado parts in a large bowl; pound delicately with a fork. Add mayonnaise and lemon juice; blend until very much mixed. Mix in crab, 3 tablespoons cilantro, chives, Serrano pepper, tricks and pepper. Spoon into staying avocado parts.

2. Move to a 15x10x1-in. heating container. Sprinkle with cheddar and paprika. Sear 4-5 in. from heat until cheddar is dissolved, 3-5 minutes. Sprinkle with residual cilantro; present with lemon wedges.

77. Low Carb Gumbo Recipe

Cook Time 1 hour Total Time 1 hour Servings: 8

INGREDIENTS:

- 12 oz. Andouille wiener (cut meagerly)
- 2 huge Bell peppers (diced; I utilized red and green)
- 1/2 huge Onion (diced)
- 1/2 cup Celery (diced)
- 4 cloves Garlic (minced)
- 8 cups Chicken stock
- 14.5-oz can Diced tomatoes (with fluid)
- tbsp. Cajun preparing (start with 1 tbsp. on the off chance that you don't need zesty)
- 1/2 tsp. Sea salt (to taste)
- 24 oz. Cauliflower rice (new or frozen)

- 12 oz. Medium shrimp (stripped and deveined, defrosted whenever frozen)
- 1-3 tsp. File powder

GUIDELINES:

1. In a little skillet over medium heat, cook the okra for around 5 minutes, until any ooze cooks away.
2. Heat the oil in an enormous Dutch oven over medium heat. Add the ringer peppers, onions, and celery. Sauté for 5-8 minutes, until the vegetables are delicate.
3. Add the cut wiener. Sauté for around 5 minutes, until browned.
4. Make a well in the middle and add the minced garlic. Allow it to sizzle for around 30 seconds, until fragrant; at that point mix in with all the other things.
5. Add the chicken stock, diced tomatoes, and sautéed okra. Season with Cajun preparing and ocean salt to taste.
6. Heat the gumbo to the point of boiling, at that point cover and stew for 30 minutes.
7. Add the shrimp. Stew for 5 minutes.

8. Add the cauliflower rice. Stew for 5 minutes once more, until shrimp is murky and cauliflower rice is delicate.

9. Eliminate from heat. Sprinkle gumbo with record powder and mix, until thickened.

Conclusion

I might want to thank you for picking this book. Hope all of you loved the best meals recipes. These recipes are appropriate for certain hypertension patients and these will ask you to diminish the sodium in your eating routine and eat an arrangement of food sources well off in supplements that help lower beat, similar to potassium, calcium and magnesium and furthermore help in weight decrease. These recipes will help you in making heavenly meals at home moreover. Plan for yourself, your relatives and appreciate. Best of luck!

CPSIA information can be obtained
at www.ICGtesting.com
Printed in the USA
BVHW061044020621
608544BV00004B/1299